THE HAIRY BIKERS
CHICKEN&EGG

THE HAIRY BIKERS
CHICKEN&EGG

We'd like to dedicate this book to our mothers – Stella and Margaret. They introduced us to the joys of chicken and to our daily chucky egg, and they started us on a wonderful journey that's led from our childhood kitchens to travels worldwide. We've been lucky. Thanks our mams.

First published in Great Britain in 2016 by
Orion Publishing Group Ltd
Carmelite House
50 Victoria Embankment
London EC4Y 0DZ
An Hachette UK Company

10 9 8 7 6 5 4 3 2 1

Text copyright © Bytebrook Limited and Sharpletter Limited 2016
Design and layout copyright © Orion 2016

A CIP catalogue record for this book is available from the British Lib

ISBN: 978 0 2976 0933 9

Photographer: Andrew Hayes-Watkins
Food director: Catherine Phipps
Food stylists: Anna Burges-Lumsden, Lisa Harrison
Design and art direction: Abi Hartshorne
Project editor: Jinny Johnson
Prop stylist: Sarah Birks
Food stylists' assistant: Lou Kenny
Proofreader: Elise See-Tai
Indexer: Vicki Robinson

Additional photos: pages 7, 39, 175, 219, 273 © BBC/Jack Coathupe; page 129 © BBC/Rosa Brough; page 179 © BBC/Chloé Juyon

Chicken and egg illustrations: © BBC/Robin Littlewood
Technique illustrations on pages 366-370: Kuo Kang Chen

Printed and bound in Germany.

The Orion Publishing Group's policy is to use papers that are natural, renewable and recyclable and made from wood grown in sustainable forests. The logging and manufacturing processes are expected to conform to the environmental regulations of the country of origin.
www.orionbooks.co.uk

BBC and the BBC logo are trademarks of the British Broadcasting Corporation and are used under licence. BBC logo © BBC 1996.

CONTENTS

CHICKEN & EGG

Everyone loves chicken – perhaps the most versatile and healthy of meats – and eggs too! Both can be turned into an almost endless variety of great-tasting dishes.

This cookbook is a real passion project for us. In fact, we first started thinking about it nearly ten years ago, so now we're really egg-cited to bring you our very best chicken and egg recipes. We have so many fantastic Hairy ideas to share and we've included easy suppers, family favourites, healthy salads and grills, as well as some special blow-out treats. So, let's do the funky chicken and get cooking...

Chicken, oh how we love it! Its mild flavour marries so well with the spices and herbs of every kind of cuisine, and it can be roasted, grilled, baked, fried, barbecued, put in a soup, a salad or a pie. Chicken is enjoyed by everybody from toddlers to grannies. In survey after survey it comes out as one of the UK's best-loved foods and it's cooked worldwide too in a multitude of ways – from the cheap and cheerful offerings of chicken shops to the fanciest creations of the world's Michelin-starred restaurants.

We both cook loads of chicken dishes at home for our families and we like experimenting with curries and braises as well as the more traditional roasts and grills. And chicken has become even more of a feature on our menus in recent years while we've been watching our weight and counting calories. It's such a healthy form of protein and it's much lower in calories and fat than red meat. Did you know that half a roast chicken, without the skin, is only about 450 calories? That means you can afford to tuck into a generous portion! Chicken can be a lifesaver for dieters.

Eggs are a super-healthy food too and a great way to get your protein – a large egg is only about 80 calories, unless you're frying it in butter of course! If you've an egg in the fridge, you're never without something good to eat.

A duck was about to cross the road when a chicken looked at him and said, 'Don't do it, man. You'll never hear the end of it.'

We've been lucky enough to travel across the world to discover the very best recipes for our BBC TV series CHICKEN & EGG. From Turin to Timbuktu, everyone has a way with these two culinary treasures. We've been to countries such as Morocco, Israel, the US and France as well as lots of places in the UK to talk to experts and home cooks about their fowl favourites – and we've heard plenty of egg-cracking chicken jokes along the way!

It's been a real eye-opener to find out just how inventive you can be with two relatively humble but fantastic ingredients and we're so chuffed with all our new discoveries. We haven't forgotten the old favourites though, so you will find casseroles, pies, salads and comforting soups as well, not forgetting a nice clutch of sweet and savoury egg dishes.

OUR FAVOURITE BIRD

A whole roast chicken is a joy to behold, with its golden crispy skin and succulent flesh, but we also have lots of recipes for pieces of chicken in this book. Of course, you can buy chicken breasts, thighs and legs for use in these dishes, but a much more economical way of going about things is to buy a whole chicken and ask your butcher to joint it for you or even do it yourself – it's easy (see page 370). You'll find this is a much cheaper option and you can use all the little scraps and trimmings in a stock. Just chuck them in a bag in the freezer until you have enough. No waste! One of the great things about chicken is you can use every bit and we make a point of doing so as a mark of respect to the animal.

Of course everyone has their favourite part of the bird – some like the dark meat of the thighs and legs; others insist on white breast meat. We think the little nuggets known as oysters that lie either side of the backbone are the best of all and we have been know to sneak a mouthful of them while carving.

When cooking pieces of chicken, be sure to choose the right cut for the recipe. For quick pan-frying or grilling, breasts are fine – although you may like to butterfly them (see page 368) to make sure they cook evenly. For slow-cooked dishes, such as curries, thighs are much more suitable. It's almost impossible to overcook a thigh and the meat is really juicy and tasty. When you do use breasts for slower-cooked dishes, it's best to have them on the bone. That will help them stay moist. We have some minced chicken recipes too and we recommend using half breast, half thigh meat for the best results.

Dave

"When I was a lad, a roast chicken dinner on a Sunday was a special treat. My mum would bung in some Packet stuffing and cook the chicken in a big enamel casserole dish until the meat was falling off the bones. We'd eat it with mash, cauli cheese and lots of gravy while listening to 'Two-way Family Favourites' on the radio. Then the next day there'd be cold chicken with bubble and squeak, and on the third a chicken soup made with the carcass and any pickings. That was three meals for the three of us – a chicken did us proud. As did my daily chucky egg. I was a scrambled kid in more ways than one, but for me, buttery scrambled eggs on golden toast was, and still is, a bit of heaven."

Si

"My mum was a great cook and she cooked chicken often. Her chicken soup was epic – she would add split peas as well as onions, carrots and potatoes and it tasted amazing. But best of all was her chicken and ham pie. She would use the dark chicken meat and ham hock so the pie was juicy and flavoursome, and she'd sometimes add leeks too. I can still remember the scent of the pie baking in the oven – it would fill the house and tempt the tastebuds like nothing else. We always had a sit-down dinner on a Saturday afternoon, when my brother came back from football, and that dinner was usually chicken pie. Even once we were all grown up we would head home for Saturday dinner with Mum. For me, the smell of chicken cooking brings back those days and will always mean home."

HOW TO BUY CHICKEN

Back when we were kids chicken was a special treat, but now we eat it any day of the week. This is thanks to the massive changes in chicken farming, with huge numbers of fast-growing broilers (birds bred for meat) being produced, bringing prices down and making chicken accessible to everyone. Also, it's now so easy to buy pieces of chicken such as breasts, thighs, drumsticks – whatever you need. When money is tight, chicken can come to the rescue, as a little can go a long way and there are plenty of recipes like this in our book.

We've often been a bit confused about all the different kinds of chicken and what the terms mean so we've done a bit of research on the whole business.

There's no doubt that you do get what you pay for with chicken and there is more flavour in free-range bird that has had a chance to move around more and had a more active, less stressful life than your basic broiler. Intensively reared birds have short lives and are fattened up quickly. Free-range birds live longer so the skeleton has a chance to grow properly, giving strength and flavour to the bones. Exercise allows the leg muscles to develop, making tastier flesh. But of course these birds are more expensive to produce because they need more space and more time.

That said, all chicken in the UK is very strictly regulated and if you buy British you are assured of a good standard. What you go for depends on your budget and on what you are cooking. For a roast or a braise, the extra flavour and better texture of the higher-welfare birds makes a difference, but how much do you notice this in a curry? Get the best you can afford and cook it carefully and you'll have a meal to enjoy.

QUICK GUIDE TO CHICKEN

BARN-REARED

These are intensively reared chickens kept indoors in large numbers in huge sheds. They may or may not have natural light in the shed and they are slaughtered at 40 days.

FREEDOM FOOD

These chickens are still reared indoors in sheds but they do have some natural light and some habitat enrichment – for instance, perches or bales to climb on. They are kept at a lower density than barn-reared birds and aren't slaughtered until they're a minimum of 56 days old.

FREE-RANGE

These birds also live in sheds but at a lower density than barn-reared. They must be allowed to spend at least half their life outdoors and can go out of the shed into pasture during daylight hours. Free-range breeders are required to allow an acre of pasture per 1,000 birds. The chickens are then slaughtered at a minimum of 56 days.

ORGANIC

Like free-range birds, organic chickens live longer lives and have to have access to the outdoors. The difference is that these birds are fed on an organic diet.

You might also see the names poulet de Bresse and corn-fed chicken. Poulet de Bresse comes from the area around Bourg-en-Bresse in southeastern France. These chickens are reared as free-range to strict regulations and fed an extra-rich diet for the last couple of weeks of their lives. This makes the flesh particularly succulent and gives a deep gamey flavour. Corn-fed chickens are fed on corn and maize and their skin is bright yellow.

CHICKEN SAFETY

One of the reasons why you have to be so careful with chicken is that raw chicken is often contaminated with a bacteria called campylobacter - the most common cause of food poisoning in the UK. As long as the chicken is handled hygienically and cooked thoroughly, campylobacter poses little problem, but it is essential to note the guidelines below. Follow these simple rules and you can enjoy your delicious chicken with no problems.

Fresh raw chicken can go off quickly so be sure to store it in the fridge, being careful that it does not contaminate other foods. Remove the chicken from any plastic wrapping and put in on a plate or in a bowl. Cover and store it at the bottom of the fridge so any juices cannot drip on to other items. It's particularly important to keep raw chicken well away from foods that will be eaten uncooked - such as cheese, fruit and salads.

- One of the worst things you can do is to wash raw chicken. This can cause any bacteria on the surface of the chicken to splash around your kitchen and spread germs on to other surfaces - and you.

- Wash chopping boards, knives and other utensils very carefully as soon as you have finished preparing raw chicken and before using them for anything else. And wash your hands thoroughly with soap and water.

- Always check that chicken is cooked through and no sign of pinkness remains. To be sure, check the internal temp with a food thermometer. It should be 73.9°C. When cooking a whole bird, check the thickest part of the leg.

- If you have leftover chicken, allow it to cool down before putting it in the fridge. It should be fine for a couple of days but be guided by the smell. If it smells off, don't eat it.

- When reheating chicken, make sure it is good and hot throughout.

- Freeze chicken on the day of purchase. To defrost, transfer the chicken to the fridge.

THE NOT SO HUMBLE EGG

Eggs are nature's little packages of goodness and one of the most nutritious and healthy of all foods. They are easy to digest and full of protein, vitamins and minerals. At one time, we were all scared off eating eggs by warnings of high cholesterol, but now the medics have decided that they are not a problem and have lifted the limits. Happy days!

Eggs are an essential ingredient in so many dishes such as cakes, batters, pastry and sauces. And of course they make a great meal in themselves. What could be nicer than a couple of perfectly poached eggs on a slice of toast or a boiled egg with buttered soldiers on the side? Eggs are used in more elaborate dishes too, such as soufflés and omelettes, and in many mousses and meringues and other great puds.

There was a major scare about eggs and salmonella bacteria in the past but this risk is now greatly reduced. Since 1998, all British Lion eggs – marked with the little red lion symbol on the eggs themselves or on the box – come from hens vaccinated against salmonella.

TYPES OF EGG

Like chicken, eggs are produced in various ways so here are our rough guidelines.

CAGE SYSTEM

The old-style battery cages have now been banned in the UK and have been replaced by larger systems known as colony cages. Birds are still kept indoors but have a bit more room to move around in, plus perching and scratching space.

BARN

The hens are kept indoors in large barns or sheds but can move around inside the barn and have more space and perches.

FREE-RANGE

Hens are kept in similar shelters to barn hens but they must have access to outside runs during daylight hours. The maximum density for free-range birds is 2,500 birds per hectare.

ORGANIC

Birds are kept in the same conditions as free-range but are fed an organic diet.

STORING EGGS

One of the main things to consider about eggs is their freshness. Because nature has given them such great packaging it's easy to forget that eggs can go off just like any other food. Fresh eggs are tastier and the whites are thicker, making them easier to cook. This is particularly important for poaching and with a fresh egg there's less risk of ending up with a nasty mess in the bottom of the pan.

According to EU regulations the date stamped on your egg or egg box should be 28 days from laying. There's an easy way to check the freshness of your eggs if you want: place the egg in a bowl of water. If it lies on its side it's very fresh. If it lies at a slight angle it's okay but past its best. If it stands vertically it's old, and if it floats, chuck it out. The reason for this is that the air sac inside the egg gets bigger as the egg gets older and so helps it float.

Official advice is to store eggs in the fridge but many people disagree and say that it spoils their flavour. If you do keep your eggs in the fridge, store them in the box as otherwise they can absorb the smells of other food through their shells.

For some recipes it helps for eggs to be at room temperature – if you're boiling eggs, for example, they may crack if added to boiling water straight from the fridge. For baking, too, it's a good idea to use room-temperature eggs as they bind better with the other ingredients.

Whole eggs cannot be frozen but egg whites freeze well. So if you're making a recipe with lots of egg yolks, stash the whites away in the freezer to use for meringues another day.

A FEW LITTLE NOTES FROM US . . .

- Peel onions, garlic and other veg and fruit unless otherwise specified.

- Use free-range eggs whenever possible. And we always use large eggs in our recipes.

- Free-range chicken does taste good but it is more expensive. Our advice is to use the best chicken you can afford. If you buy British you're assured of a decent standard of meat.

- A meat probe thermometer is a really useful bit of kit if you want to be sure of perfectly cooked chicken every time.

- Stock features in lots of recipes and we've included recipes for making your own chicken stock at the back of the book – it's not difficult and it's a great thing to have in your freezer. Otherwise, use the good fresh stocks available in supermarkets or use the little stock pots or cubes. Many are pretty good these days.

- We've made oven temperatures and cooking times as accurate as possible, but all ovens are different so keep an eye on your dish and be prepared to cook it for a longer or shorter time if necessary.

SOUPS
and SALADS

COCK-A-LEEKIE SOUP

Warming and tasty, this is a favourite Scottish chicken soup – ideal for a Burns Night supper on a cold winter's evening. The prunes are a traditional ingredient and add a lovely touch of sweetness, but it's fine to leave them out if you're not a prune fan.

SERVES 4

1 tbsp olive oil

25g butter

1 onion, finely chopped

2 carrots, diced

2 celery sticks, diced

150g turnips or swede, diced

4 leeks, 1 finely diced, 3 sliced into rings

bouquet garni made up of 2 bay leaves, 1 sprig of parsley and 1 sprig of thyme

2 chicken legs, skinned

100ml white wine

1.2 litres chicken stock

8 soft prunes, cut into quarters

100g cooked ham, diced

50ml crème fraiche

1 tbsp finely snipped chives

sea salt and freshly ground black pepper

Heat the oil and 10g of the butter in a large flameproof casserole dish and add the onion, carrots, celery, turnips or swede and the finely diced leek. Fry them gently over a medium heat, stirring regularly, for about 10 minutes until the vegetables start to take on some colour.

Add the bouquet garni and the chicken legs, then pour over the wine. Allow the wine to bubble for a couple of minutes, then add the stock. Season with salt and pepper and bring everything to the boil, then turn the heat down to a simmer and cover the pan. Simmer the soup for about 45 minutes, until the vegetables are tender and the chicken is close to falling off the bone.

Towards the end of the 45 minutes, heat the remaining butter in a frying pan and add the sliced leeks, the prunes and a splash of water. Cover the pan and cook gently for about 10 minutes until the leeks and prunes are close to tender.

Remove the chicken legs from the casserole dish and take all the meat off the bones. Add the leeks and prunes to the soup, then the ham and crème fraiche and simmer for another 10 minutes, then add the chicken to warm through. Serve with finely snipped chives.

PERUVIAN CHICKEN SOUP *with* QUINOA

Peruvian food is on-trend at the moment and super delicious. Even Paddington would have given up his marmalade sandwiches for this tasty soup. When poaching the chicken it's well worth straining the broth as we suggest. This gets rid of the starchy gunk and gives you a fresher-tasting soup.

—————————— SERVES 4-6 ——————————

1.5 litres chicken stock

4 chicken thighs or 2 chicken breasts, skin on and bone in

2 tbsp olive oil

1 onion, thinly sliced

2 celery sticks, thinly sliced

1 red pepper, deseeded and sliced

100g quinoa, rinsed and soaked for 5 minutes

2 garlic cloves, crushed

1 tbsp Amarillo chilli sauce, or similar mild chilli sauce

1 bay leaf

1 sprig of fresh oregano

1 large sweet potato, diced

large bunch of coriander, roughly chopped

lime wedges, to serve

sea salt and freshly ground black pepper

Pour the chicken stock into a large saucepan and bring it to the boil, then add the chicken. Turn the heat down low and simmer gently for about 10 minutes, until the chicken is cooked through. Skim off any foam that collects on the surface, then remove the chicken and set it aside. Strain the chicken broth through a sieve lined with a double layer of muslin or cheesecloth into a bowl and set this aside too.

Heat the olive oil in the same pan and add the onion, celery and red pepper. Cook them over a medium heat for about 5 minutes, just to start the softening process, then add the quinoa. Continue to toast the quinoa until it starts to smell nutty, then add the garlic and chilli sauce. Cook for another minute or so.

Pour the chicken stock back into the saucepan, then add the herbs and season with salt and pepper. Bring the soup to the boil, then turn the heat down and simmer for 15 minutes. Add the sweet potato and simmer for a further 5 minutes.

Remove the skin and bone from each piece of chicken and cut the flesh into slices. Add these slices to the soup and simmer for a few minutes to warm through. Taste for seasoning and add more if necessary. Remove the bay leaf and oregano, then stir in the chopped coriander. Serve in bowls with lime wedges on the side.

THAI CHICKEN SOUP

The proper name for this soup is 'tom kha gai'. We like it spicy and our recipe is just right for us, but cut down the chillies if they're too much for you. This is great as a soup, but you could also serve it over some steamed jasmine rice for a more filling feast if you like.

SERVES 4

750ml chicken stock

400ml can of coconut milk

3 shallots, preferably red, finely sliced

25g galangal root, thinly sliced (or 1 tbsp galangal paste)

2 lemongrass stalks, white insides only, finely chopped

4 Kaffir lime leaves, finely shredded

2 or 3 bird's eye chillies, sliced (deseeded if you like)

pinch of salt

1 tsp palm sugar or light brown sugar

300g boneless, skinless chicken thighs or breast, thinly sliced

150g oyster mushrooms, wiped and sliced

juice of 1–2 limes

2–3 tbsp fish sauce

a few sprigs of fresh coriander

Pour the chicken stock and coconut milk into a large saucepan. Bring them to the boil, then add the shallots, galangal, lemongrass, lime leaves and chillies. Season with the salt and sugar.

Simmer for a few minutes, then add the chicken and mushrooms and continue to simmer until the chicken is cooked through. Add a tablespoon each of lime juice and fish sauce, then taste and add more until you get the flavour you want. The soup should be a good balance of hot, sweet, sour and salty. Sprinkle with fresh coriander before serving.

CLASSIC JEWISH CHICKEN SOUP

There are a million and one versions of this, probably the best of all chicken soups, and this is ours. It's also known as 'Jewish penicillin' and sure enough a bowlful of this really does make you feel good – almost worth getting flu for. Great with or without the matzo balls.

SERVES 4

4 chicken legs, bone in

1.5 litres chicken stock

1 large onion, cut into wedges

2 carrots, cut into chunks

2 turnips, cut into wedges

2 celery sticks, cut into chunks

large sprig of thyme

large sprig of parsley

1 bay leaf

4 garlic cloves, chopped

1 strip of lemon peel

25g angel hair pasta

2 tbsp chopped parsley or dill

sea salt and freshly ground black pepper

MATZO BALLS

100g matzo meal

2 tsp baking powder

1 tbsp finely chopped parsley or dill

grating of nutmeg

125ml chicken stock (from the soup)

50g butter, melted

1 egg, beaten

Remove the skin from the chicken legs. Put the legs in a large saucepan and pour over the stock. Season with salt and pepper, then bring the stock to the boil. Skim off any grey-looking foam that collects on the surface of the stock and keep skimming until the foam turns white.

Reduce the heat, cover the pan and simmer for 30 minutes. Add all the vegetables, then the herbs, garlic and lemon peel and simmer for 20 minutes until the vegetables are well on their way to being tender.

While the soup is cooking, make the matzo balls. Put the matzo meal and baking powder in a bowl and mix with a good pinch of salt. Stir in the parsley or dill and grate in a little nutmeg. Mix the stock and butter together and add them to the bowl, along with the beaten egg. Mix thoroughly, then leave the mixture to stand for half an hour so the matzo meal can absorb all the liquid.

Divide the mixture into balls of about 20g each - the size of a small walnut. Bring a saucepan of water to the boil and season it with salt. Carefully add the balls to the water and simmer them very gently for 10-12 minutes until they are cooked through, then drain.

Take the chicken legs out of the soup. When they are cool enough to handle, remove the meat from the bones, keeping it in fairly large pieces. Add the meat to the soup. Break up the pasta into short lengths and add them to the soup, along with the matzo balls. Continue to simmer until the pasta is cooked and the matzo balls are warmed through. This should only take a couple of minutes.

Taste the soup and adjust the seasoning to taste, then remove the sprigs of herbs and the lemon peel. Sprinkle with parsley or dill before serving.

CHICKEN *and* DUMPLING STEW

You don't need a lot of chicken for this, as the stew is bulked out with fab dumplings. Top tip: add a teaspoonful of dried sage to the dumpling mix if you fancy – it tastes great. This is the best-ever dish to serve up on a cold evening. Warms the cockles of your heart.

SERVES 4

1 tbsp olive oil

50g bacon lardons (optional)

1 large onion, diced

2 carrots, diced

2 celery sticks, diced

150g swede, diced

3 turnips or 1 large parsnip, diced

1.2 litres chicken stock

1 bay leaf

sprig of thyme

sprig of parsley

1 large potato, diced

2 leeks, cut into rounds

¼ savoy cabbage or similar, shredded

250g cooked chicken

sea salt and freshly ground black pepper

DUMPLINGS

200g self-raising flour

1 tsp baking powder

100g shredded suet

Heat the olive oil in a large, flameproof casserole dish. Add the bacon, if using, and fry it until crisp and brown, then add the onion, carrots, celery, swede and the turnips or parsnip. Sauté everything over a medium heat for about 10 minutes, stirring regularly, until the vegetables have started to soften and brown. Pour in the chicken stock and add the herbs, then season with salt and pepper and simmer for 10 minutes.

Add the potato, leeks and cabbage to the soup. Simmer for a further 20 minutes, then stir in the cooked chicken. Preheat the oven to 200°C/ Fan 180°C/Gas 6.

To make the dumplings, put the flour in a bowl with the baking powder and season with salt and pepper. Stir in the suet, then add enough cold water to make a sticky dough – you'll need at least 100ml. Divide the dough into about 8 or more rough pieces – it will be sticky and won't form neat balls.

Drop the dumplings on top of the stew, then put the casserole dish in the oven for 20 minutes until the dumplings are well risen and browned slightly on top. Serve piping hot.

PORTUGUESE CHICKEN SOUP
with mint and lime

Known as 'canja', this is a popular soup in Portugal and Brazil and really makes the best of every bit of flavour from the chicken. We usually make it with chicken pieces but you can poach a whole bird if you like and make a really big batch.

1.5 litres well-flavoured chicken stock

2 skinless chicken thighs or 1 breast, bone in

a few sprigs of mint

small bunch of parsley

1 bay leaf

2 large strips of thinly pared lime zest

2 garlic cloves, finely sliced

150g basmati rice or orzo

lime or lemon wedges, to serve

sea salt

Pour the chicken stock into a large saucepan and bring it to the boil, then add the chicken. Turn the heat down low and simmer gently for about 10 minutes, until the chicken is cooked through. Skim off any foam that collects on the surface. Remove the chicken and set it aside. Strain the chicken broth through a sieve lined with a double layer of muslin or cheesecloth into a bowl, then pour it back into the saucepan.

Reheat the chicken stock. Strip the nicest leaves from the mint sprigs and set them aside for later. Add the rest of the mint and a few sprigs of the parsley to the broth with the bay leaf, lime zest and garlic slices. Season with salt. Rinse the rice, if using, then add this or the orzo to the broth and simmer for 10–12 minutes. Remove the sprigs of mint and parsley and the bay leaf and zest.

Remove the skin and bones from the chicken and cut the flesh into thin slices. Add them to the soup with the rest of the parsley, finely chopped. Put some of the reserved mint leaves in your soup bowls and ladle the soup over them, then sprinkle over a few more mint leaves. Serve with lime or lemon wedges.

CREAM *of* CHICKEN SOUP

A lovely rich creamy soup, this is a great thing to make with any leftover chicken from your Sunday roast, or you can cook or buy a chicken breast. After tasting this you'll never open another tin.

SERVES 4

25g butter

1 onion, finely chopped

2 leeks, white part only, finely chopped

1 celery stick, finely chopped

1 medium potato, finely diced

bouquet garni made up of 1 bay leaf, 1 sprig of parsley and 1 sprig of tarragon

500ml chicken stock

300ml whole milk

150–200g leftover roast chicken or a large chicken breast, cooked and diced

75ml double cream (the pouring sort)

1 egg yolk

a few snipped chives or finely chopped parsley, to serve

sea salt and freshly ground black pepper

Heat the butter in a large saucepan. When it has melted, add the onion, leeks, celery, potato and a splash of water. Fry gently over a low heat, partially covered but still stirring regularly, until the vegetables have softened, but don't let them take on any colour.

Season the vegetables with salt and pepper, then add the bouquet garni. Pour in the chicken stock and the milk. Simmer gently for about 15 minutes, until the vegetables are completely tender.

Remove the pan from the heat and allow the soup to cool slightly. Transfer it to a blender and add the cooked chicken. Blitz the soup until very smooth, then pour it back into the pan. Alternatively, you can use a stick blender if you have one and blitz the soup in the pan.

Reheat the soup gently, then check the seasoning and add salt and pepper to taste. Whisk the double cream with the egg yolk, then stir it into the soup, taking care that the soup doesn't come anywhere near boiling. Serve sprinkled with some finely snipped chives or chopped parsley.

EGG DROP SOUP

If you have some good stock to hand, this traditional Chinese soup is super quick to make and is really nourishing and comforting to eat. It's basically chicken broth with fine strands of egg cooked in it – chicken meets egg in perfect harmony and a fine bit of ying and yang.

SERVES 4

1.2 litres well-flavoured chicken stock

20g root ginger, very thinly sliced

2 garlic cloves, thinly sliced

1 star anise

a few peppercorns

6 spring onions, finely sliced

soy sauce

3 eggs

1 tsp cornflour

fresh coriander leaves

sea salt

Pour the stock into a large saucepan. Add the ginger, garlic, star anise, peppercorns and half the spring onions and season with salt. Bring the stock to the boil, then turn down the heat and simmer for 15 minutes.

Strain the soup into a clean saucepan, taste to check the seasoning and add soy sauce and extra salt to taste. Put the pan over a very low heat so the liquid is not quite simmering. Crack the eggs into a small bowl, then beat them with the cornflour until completely combined.

This next stage requires some dexterity, or a willing helper. Take a fork and hold it in place at the edge of the bowl containing the eggs. Tip the bowl, making sure the fork is pointing down so you can pour the eggs through the fork prongs. Pour the egg mixture into the broth in a steady stream, whisking gently as you do so.

Leave the soup to stand for no more than around 30 seconds while the strands of egg cook in the hot broth, then serve at once. Garnish with the remaining spring onions and some coriander leaves.

SHAY COOPER'S CHICKEN SOUP

We were lucky enough to work with Shay Cooper – executive chef at The Goring, one of London's top luxury hotels – while filming our 'Chicken and Egg' TV series. He showed us his amazing chicken soup recipe, which is truly special. At The Goring this is served with confit egg yolks, glazed mushrooms and mushroom ketchup on the side, but you'll have to go along there to enjoy those!

SERVES 6

1 tbsp rapeseed oil

2 chicken legs, 2 thighs and 2 wings, bone in and skin on

1 chicken back, cut in half

150g celery, diced

200g white onion, diced

150g leeks, diced

4 sprigs of thyme

3 sprigs of flat-leaf parsley

2 bay leaves

4 litres chicken stock

130g unsalted butter, softened

130g plain flour

150g crème fraiche

75ml dry sherry

lemon juice

sea salt and freshly ground black pepper

Heat the rapeseed oil in a heavy-based saucepan over a medium to high heat. Add the chicken and cook until it's well browned all over. Remove the chicken and set it aside. Add the celery, onion and leek to the pan and sweat for 3–5 minutes until soft and translucent.

Add the thyme, parsley and bay leaves and put the chicken back in the pan. Pour in the stock and boil gently until it's reduced by half.

Meanwhile, melt the butter in a separate pan and mix in the flour to make a smooth paste. Once the stock has reduced, stir in the butter and flour paste and simmer the soup gently for 30 minutes. Remove the pan from the heat and pass the soup through a fine sieve.

While the soup is still warm, stir in the crème fraiche and sherry and season with lemon juice, salt and pepper to taste. Serve hot.

VIETNAMESE CHICKEN SALAD

Poaching the chicken ensures the meat is good and juicy, and using lots of lovely Asian flavours gives the salad extra punch. Poaching is also a great method for cooking chicken for sandwiches. If you're pushed for time, though, you can make the salad with ready-cooked chicken instead.

SERVES 4

500ml chicken stock

2 star anise

3 garlic cloves

15g root ginger, sliced

strip of lime zest

good pinch of salt

3 skinless, boneless chicken breasts

SALAD

½ Chinese lettuce

1 carrot

½ white radish (mooli)

4 spring onions

leaves from a small bunch of fresh coriander

leaves from a small bunch of mint

DRESSING

2 tbsp fish sauce

juice of 1 lime

1 tsp rice wine vinegar

½ tsp sugar

2 red chillies, sliced

25g root ginger, finely chopped

sea salt and freshly ground pepper

First poach the chicken. Put the chicken stock in a saucepan with the star anise, garlic, ginger and lime zest. Season with the salt and simmer for 5 minutes. Add the chicken breasts, then top up the liquid with water if necessary so the chicken is completely submerged. Cover the pan and simmer the chicken for 8–10 minutes until it's just cooked through. Remove the chicken from the stock and leave it to cool slightly, then shred the meat or cut it into strips. Set the chicken aside and save the stock for something else, such as a soup.

Shred the Chinese lettuce, and cut the carrot and the white radish into matchsticks. Cut the spring onions in half and shred them lengthways.

Arrange all the salad ingredients and the chicken on a large platter or in a salad bowl. Whisk all the ingredients for the dressing in a small bowl and then taste before seasoning, as the fish sauce can be quite salty. Leave the dressing to stand for 5 minutes; then pour it over the salad and serve immediately.

CORONATION CHICKEN

An oldie but a goodie, this salad was invented in 1952 for Coronation Day and it's still much-loved today. We know there are lots of ingredients here, but there's nothing difficult about our reinvention of the classic and it doesn't take long to put together. You can add a handful of sultanas if you like.

SERVES 4

1 tbsp olive oil

4 skinless, boneless chicken breasts

grated zest and juice of 1 lemon

knob of butter

1 shallot, finely chopped

1 red chilli, deseeded and finely chopped

2 tsp Madras curry powder

2 tbsp tomato purée

100ml dry white wine

1 tbsp apricot jam

100ml chicken stock

150ml mayonnaise

75ml crème fraiche

1 large mango, flesh diced

4 spring onions, finely chopped

2 tbsp chopped fresh coriander

dash of Tabasco sauce

50g flaked almonds

sea salt and freshly ground black pepper

Rub the olive oil all over the chicken. Scatter over the lemon zest and season with salt and pepper. It's best to steam the chicken to keep it lovely and tender, so put a piece of baking parchment in the bottom of a steamer pan or a steamer insert, then add the chicken. Steam the chicken for 15 minutes, or until cooked through, then set it aside to cool.
If you don't have a steamer you could poach the chicken instead.

Melt the butter in a saucepan, add the shallot and chilli and fry for 5 minutes. Stir in the curry powder and cook for 2–3 minutes. Stir in the tomato purée and cook for a further minute. Add the wine and continue to cook until the volume of the liquid has reduced by half.

Stir in the jam and stock, then continue to simmer until the volume of the liquid has reduced by half. Take the pan off the heat and set aside to cool.

Mix the mayonnaise and the crème fraiche together in a bowl until well combined, then stir in the curry mixture. Fold in the mango, spring onions, lemon juice and coriander.

Cut the chicken into bite-sized pieces and fold them into the bowl with the other ingredients. Season with salt, pepper and Tabasco to taste. Toast the almonds in a dry frying pan and toss them over the top of the salad. Great as part of a buffet, in a sandwich or served on a baked potato.

BANG BANG CHICKEN SALAD

This is one of the best salads ever. It's amazing as a starter, a main meal or as part of a buffet and it's one of those dishes you just can't stop eating. Boom bang-a-bang!

2 skinless, boneless chicken breasts

1 tbsp soy sauce

2 garlic cloves, crushed

15g root ginger, grated

1 tsp sesame oil

½ tsp Chinese five-spice powder

sea salt and freshly ground black pepper

SAUCE

1 tbsp vegetable oil

2 shallots, finely chopped

2 garlic cloves, crushed or grated

15g root ginger, grated

2 red chillies, deseeded if you like, and finely chopped

200ml chicken stock

150ml coconut milk

50g crunchy peanut butter

1 tbsp soy sauce

1 tbsp rice wine vinegar

1 tsp palm sugar or light soft brown sugar

juice of ½ lime

First butterfly the chicken breasts (see page 368) and cut them in half. Put the pieces in a bowl and season them with salt and pepper. Mix the soy sauce, garlic, ginger, sesame oil and five-spice together in a small jug, then pour it over the chicken and massage it in well. Leave the chicken to marinate while you make the sauce.

For the sauce, heat the vegetable oil in a frying pan and add the shallots. Cook for a few minutes over a medium heat until the shallots are golden brown, then add the garlic, ginger and chillies. Cook for a couple more minutes, add the chicken stock, coconut milk and peanut butter, then the soy sauce, rice wine vinegar, sugar and lime juice. Simmer until the sauce is reduced and syrupy, then set aside.

To cook the chicken, heat a griddle until it's very hot. Decant 2 or 3 tablespoons of the peanut sauce into a separate bowl so you don't contaminate it all with raw chicken, and use this to brush over the chicken. Put the chicken on the griddle and cook for 3-4 minutes on each side, basting with more of the sauce as you go. The chicken should have black char lines and look lightly glazed.

SALAD

1 Chinese cabbage

1 large carrot

50g radishes

1 red pepper

100g baby corn

100g asparagus tips

6 spring onions

TO SERVE

2 or 3 red chillies,
sliced into rounds

small bunch of
fresh coriander

For the salad, shred the cabbage, then cut the carrot and radishes into matchsticks and the pepper into thin strips. Quarter the baby corn, cut the asparagus diagonally into short pieces and shred the spring onions.

Arrange all the salad ingredients on a serving platter. Cut the chicken into strips and allow them to cool a little, then add them to the salad. Drizzle over some of the remaining peanut dressing and sprinkle with more red chillies and coriander leaves. Serve any leftover sauce at the table.

GRIDDLED CHICKEN SALAD

We're both big fans of Caesar salad with its croutons and egg dressing, so we've combined that style with griddled chicken and come up with a real winner. Perhaps if Caesar had had our recipe, his Empire would never have fallen. Hope you love this as much as we do.

SERVES 4

2 boneless, skinless chicken breasts

1 tbsp olive oil

1 tsp dried thyme

sea salt and freshly ground black pepper

CROUTONS

½ ciabatta loaf

4 tbsp olive oil

2 garlic cloves, sliced

2 tbsp finely chopped parsley

DRESSING

4 anchovy fillets, finely chopped

1 garlic clove, crushed

1 tsp Dijon mustard

juice of ½ lemon

4 tbsp olive oil

SALAD

1 large cos or heart of romaine lettuce

12 cherry tomatoes, halved (optional)

25g Parmesan cheese, finely grated

1 egg yolk

Butterfly the chicken breasts (see page 368), then put them in a bowl and season with salt and pepper. Drizzle the chicken with the oil and sprinkle over the thyme, then leave it to marinate for an hour. Heat a griddle pan until it's too hot to hold your hand over and griddle the chicken for 3–4 minutes on each side until cooked through and lightly charred. Set the chicken aside to cool, then cut it into strips.

To make the croutons, cut the bread into small cubes. Heat the oil in a frying pan and add the garlic slices. Fry until the garlic is on the verge of turning brown, then quickly remove it from the pan with a slotted spoon and discard. Add the bread and stir to coat it all with the garlicky oil. Sauté, stirring regularly, until the bread is crisp, slightly glossy and golden brown. Add the parsley and stir for another minute, then take the pan off the heat.

To make the dressing, put the anchovies, garlic and Dijon mustard in the bottom of your salad bowl. Whisk in the lemon juice, then the oil and check for seasoning. The anchovies will be salty but you can add salt and pepper to taste.

When you're ready to serve the salad, add the lettuce to the bowl, along with the tomatoes, if using. Add the chicken, then sprinkle over the grated Parmesan. Drop the egg yolk into the bowl, then toss everything together. Stir in the croutons and serve immediately.

CHICKEN LIVER SALAD
with oranges and little gems

Chicken livers are cheap to buy and good to eat and we love 'em. The sharp, spicy, citrusy dressing works so well in this salad and you can add more veggies if you like.

SERVES 4

2 oranges

2 tbsp olive oil

400g chicken livers, rinsed, trimmed and cut into bite-sized pieces

1 tsp cinnamon

½ tsp ground allspice

½ tsp ground cumin

½ tsp cayenne

juice of ½ lemon

2 tsp sherry vinegar

1 tsp Dijon mustard

4 little gem lettuces

½ red onion, finely sliced

small bunch of parsley, finely chopped (optional)

sea salt

First prepare the oranges. Top and tail one of them, then stand it upright and cut the skin away, taking all the pith and membrane with it. Cut the orange flesh into rounds, removing any seeds as you go, and set them aside for later. Squeeze the juice from the discarded peel into a bowl. Repeat with the second orange.

Heat a tablespoon of the oil in a frying pan. Season the chicken livers with salt and add them to the pan. Sprinkle over the spices and toss to coat all the livers, then fry them for 3-4 minutes on each side, until just cooked. Remove the livers from the pan and leave them to cool slightly.

Add the lemon juice to the orange juice and whisk in the vinegar. Add the rest of the olive oil and the mustard to the frying pan, heat for a minute, then pour the juices and vinegar into the pan as well. Stir to combine, making sure you scrape up any nice sticky bits from the bottom of the pan.

Slice the little gems into quarters - or eighths if they are large. Put them on a serving platter with the orange and onion slices and add the livers. Pour over the dressing, then sprinkle with the parsley, if using.

SMOKED CHICKEN SALAD *with peaches*

Chicken is great smoked and it goes brilliantly with fruit. This makes a tasty starter or a light lunch, but if you want something more filling, you could use two smoked chicken breasts or add some chunky grain such as spelt. This recipe works well with smoked duck too.

SERVES 4

1 large smoked chicken breast

200g salad leaves, such as lamb's lettuce, pea shoots and baby kale

2 ripe peaches, cut into wedges

50g pecans, lightly toasted

½ cucumber

fresh thyme or oregano leaves

DRESSING

1 tsp wholegrain mustard

2 tbsp olive oil

pinch of sugar

1 tbsp sherry vinegar

a few rosemary leaves, very finely chopped

sea salt and freshly ground black pepper

Slice the chicken as thinly as you can. Arrange the salad leaves on a large platter and top with slices of chicken, peach wedges and pecans. Peel and deseed the cucumber and cut it into little crescents, then add those to the platter.

Whisk the dressing ingredients in a small jug and season with salt and pepper to taste. Drizzle the dressing over the salad, then sprinkle the herbs on top.

CHICKEN, AVOCADO *and* BEAN SALAD

Chicken and avocado are perfect partners and with the addition of beans and a spritz of lime they make a wonderful Mexican-inspired salad. What's not to like? This tastes as good as it looks.

SERVES 4

2 skinless, boneless chicken breasts

1 tbsp olive oil

1 tbsp chipotle paste

juice of ½ lime

2 avocados, cut into chunks

400g can of black beans, drained and rinsed

½ red onion, sliced

1 large red pepper, diced

200g cherry tomatoes, halved

3 little gem lettuces or 1 heart of romaine lettuce, shredded

large handful of fresh coriander leaves

sea salt and freshly ground black pepper

DRESSING

2 tbsp olive oil

juice of 1 lime

1 tsp red wine vinegar

pinch of sugar

pinch of cumin

pinch of oregano

Butterfly the chicken breasts (see page 368). Season the chicken with salt and pepper, then whisk the olive oil with chipotle paste and rub this mixture over the chicken. Heat a griddle to a medium heat.

Grill the chicken for 3 or 4 minutes on each side until cooked through with good char lines. Leave the chicken to cool to room temperature, then cut it into slices.

Put the lime juice in a large bowl and add the chunks of avocado. Stir very gently just to coat the avocado in the juice, then sprinkle with salt. Add the beans and the rest of the salad ingredients, including the chicken.

Whisk the dressing ingredients together in a small jug and season with salt and pepper. Pour the dressing over the salad and toss everything together gently before serving.

MEDITERRANEAN CHICKEN SALAD

The smell of fresh basil always transports us to the Mediterranean and this is a perfect salad for a summer's day. You can use roasted peppers from a jar so your lunch is on the table in no time. Every bite is a sunshine holiday.

SERVES 4

2 skinless, boneless chicken breasts

1 tbsp olive oil

zest and juice of ½ lemon

1 garlic clove, crushed

1 large courgette

100g rocket leaves

2 roasted red peppers, cut into strips (from a jar is fine)

handful of basil leaves

sea salt and freshly ground black pepper

DRESSING

50g sundried tomatoes

3 tbsp olive oil

1 tsp Italian herbs or herbes de Provence

1 tsp lemon zest and juice of ½ lemon

2 tsp red wine vinegar

25g black olives, pitted

Butterfly the chicken breasts (see page 368) and cut them in half. Mix the olive oil with the lemon zest and juice in a bowl and add the garlic. Season with salt and pepper, then add the chicken and leave it to marinate for a few minutes.

Meanwhile, cut the courgette into long slices on the diagonal. Heat a griddle until it's too hot to hold your hand over. Grill the courgette slices for 2 or 3 minutes on each side, until they're slightly softened and marked with char lines. Set them aside and turn the heat down to medium.

Griddle the pieces of chicken for 3-4 minutes on each side – you might need to do this in batches. Remove the chicken, check it is cooked through and leave it to rest for 5 minutes. Cut it into slices.

Arrange the rocket leaves on a platter and top with the roasted red peppers, courgette slices and chicken.

Make the dressing by blitzing all the ingredients together in a food processor, then season with salt and pepper. If the dressing is too thick to spoon over the salad (you want something slightly looser than dropping consistency), add a little water to thin it out.

Sprinkle the basil over the salad, then add the dressing. Serve at once.

SAVOURY
EGGS

CLASSIC FRENCH OMELETTE

The secret to a good French omelette is cooking it in butter. For a touch of trad French oh là là, try the herby filling, known as 'omelette fines herbes', but we love our northern variation with black pudding too. A cracker, we promise you.

SERVES 1

3 eggs

10g butter

sea salt and freshly ground black pepper

HERB FILLING

1 tbsp each of chopped parsley, chervil, tarragon and chives

BLACK PUDDING FILLING

10g butter

½ onion, finely chopped

½ small apple, cored and finely diced

75g black pudding, skinned

To make a plain omelette, crack the eggs into a bowl, season them with salt and pepper, then break them up lightly with a fork. Melt the butter in a frying pan until it's bubbling. Pour in the eggs and wait a few seconds for the underside of the omelette to set, then start working the edges into the centre with a fork, letting the liquid egg fill the gaps.

Continue to cook the omelette to your liking. A fairly runny omelette will be ready in about a minute; double this for a well-done, firm omelette. Flip one side of the omelette towards the centre, then follow with the other side and slide it on to a plate. Serve at once.

For the herb omelette, mix the herbs together and reserve a scant tablespoon. Mix the rest of the herbs with the eggs and proceed as above. Sprinkle the finished omelette with the reserved herbs.

For the black pudding omelette, heat the butter in a small frying pan. Add the onion and apple and fry them over a medium heat for a few minutes until lightly browned and softened. Crumble up the black pudding and add it to the pan. Keep frying until the black pudding has crisped up a little, then set the pan aside. Make the omelette as described above, but when the eggs are almost set, add the filling in a line down the centre and fold the sides over it before turning out on to a plate.

CHILLI *and* GARLIC OMELETTE

This is a slender little omelette but with chilli, garlic and spices it has bags of flavour. It's just the thing to wake you up on a Sunday morning or for any time you need a spicy egg fix.

1 tbsp olive oil

2 spring onions, finely chopped

2 garlic cloves, finely chopped

10g root ginger, finely chopped

1 red chilli, deseeded and finely chopped (or sliced – up to you)

2 eggs, beaten

generous pinch of turmeric

½ tsp garam masala or curry powder

a few sprigs of fresh coriander

sea salt

Heat the olive oil in a frying pan. Add the spring onions and fry them for just a couple of minutes – you want them to have some bite. Add the garlic, ginger and chilli and stir for another minute.

Crack the eggs into a bowl and add the turmeric, garam masala and a good pinch of salt. Whisk briefly, then pour the mixture into the frying pan and swirl it around so it completely covers the base of the pan. Let the omelette cook through, then sprinkle it with coriander and slide it on to a plate. If you prefer, roll the omelette up first, then transfer it to a plate. Eat at once.

EGG FOO YUNG

This Chinese omelette is a take-away favourite, but we think our home-made version tastes even better. Try adding some leftover chicken if you fancy, as this is a recipe where chicken and egg work well together. You don't have to make the sauce but you'll be extra happy if you do.

SERVES 4

2 tbsp vegetable oil

150g minced pork

4 spring onions,
finely chopped

2 garlic cloves,
finely chopped

25g root ginger,
finely chopped

2 tbsp soy sauce

1 tbsp mirin

½ tsp sesame oil

150g raw shelled
prawns, cut up

100g bean sprouts,
cut in half

1 carrot, peeled
and shredded

small bunch of fresh
coriander, chopped

6 eggs, beaten

sea salt and freshly
ground black pepper

SAUCE

300ml chicken stock

30ml soy sauce

30ml oyster sauce

2 garlic cloves,
finely chopped

25g root ginger,
finely chopped

½ tsp chilli flakes

¼ tsp brown sugar

1 tsp cornflour

If you are serving the sauce, make that first. Put the stock in a saucepan with the soy sauce, oyster sauce, garlic, ginger, chilli flakes and sugar. Stir to combine and heat through. Mix the cornflour with a little water to make a smooth paste, then add this to the sauce. Stir over a gentle heat until the sauce has thickened very slightly – it should look syrupy. Taste and adjust the seasoning if necessary. Set the sauce aside and keep it warm in a low oven.

To make the omelette, heat a tablespoon of oil in a frying pan. When it's hot, add the minced pork, spring onions, garlic and ginger. Fry quickly until the pork is browned all over and just cooked through. Pour in the soy sauce and mirin, with 2 tablespoons of water and simmer for a couple of minutes, until the liquid has reduced. Drizzle over the sesame oil, then remove the pan from the heat and leave to cool a little.

Put the raw prawns, bean sprouts, carrot and coriander in a bowl. Add the eggs and season with salt and pepper, then stir in the pork mixture.

Heat your grill to medium hot. Heat the rest of the oil in a large frying pan. Pour the mixture into the pan and cook until the underside is well browned, then pop the pan under the hot grill so the omelette can finish cooking. Cut the omelette into quarters to serve.

CLASSIC FRITTATA

A frittata is an Italian omelette and it's very quick and easy to make. It's great filled with peas and beans and lots of herbs, but once you've got the hang of it you can experiment with other veggies. The ricotta on the top adds extra lusciousness.

SERVES 4

1 tbsp olive oil

1 large courgette, thinly sliced

1 garlic clove, finely chopped

100g frozen peas

50g frozen baby broad beans

zest of ½ lemon

6 eggs

small handful of basil leaves, roughly chopped

small handful of mint leaves, roughly chopped

100g ricotta cheese

sea salt and freshly ground black pepper

Preheat your grill to medium. Heat the olive oil in a large frying pan. Add the courgette and fry it gently over a medium heat until softened and slightly browned round the edges. Add the garlic and cook for a further minute.

Bring a pan of salted water to the boil, add the peas and beans and blanch them for 2 minutes. Drain, then add them to the pan with the courgettes. Add the lemon zest.

Beat the eggs in a bowl, season them with salt and pepper, then pour them over the contents of the frying pan. Sprinkle the basil and mint leaves into the pan, then dot teaspoons of ricotta over the eggs.

Cook the frittata for several minutes over a low to medium heat until the underside is cooked but the mixture is still wobbly in the middle. Put the pan under the grill for a couple of minutes, keeping an eye on it so the top doesn't catch. The frittata will puff up, but will subside again as it cools.

Transfer the frittata to a plate and serve in wedges with some salad. Tastes best at room temperature.

OMELETTE ARNOLD BENNETT

We've done a dieters' version of this famous smoked haddock omelette, created by the Savoy Hotel for the novelist Arnold Bennett, in the past, but this is the full monty. Lucky old Arnold, we say. For the ultimate in posh egg dishes, swap the haddock for poached lobster.

SERVES 2

250ml whole milk

slice of onion

1 mace blade

1 bay leaf

a few peppercorns

250g smoked haddock or other smoked fish

10g butter

5 eggs

25g grated Gruyère (or other hard cheese)

a few chives, snipped

sea salt and freshly ground black pepper

SAUCE

30g butter

30g flour

reserved poaching liquid

100ml double cream

Put the milk in a saucepan that's wide enough to hold the fish in a single layer. Add the onion, mace, bay leaf and peppercorns and bring the milk to just under the boil. Remove the pan from the heat and leave the milk to infuse for half an hour.

Just before you want to cook the fish, bring the milk to the boil. Add the fish, remove the pan from the heat and cover it with a lid. Leave for about 5 minutes until the fish has cooked through and flakes easily. Remove the fish from the pan with a slotted spoon and set it aside, then strain the poaching milk into a jug.

Next make the sauce. Melt the 30g of butter in a saucepan, then stir in the flour and mix well. Stir over the heat for a few minutes to cook the flour. Gradually pour in the reserved poaching milk, stirring in between each addition, until it is all added. Then add the cream, continuing to stir until you have a fairly thick sauce.

Take the pan off the heat, flake the fish and stir it into the sauce. Taste for seasoning and add a little more salt if necessary – you may not need it as the fish will be salty. Cover the pan and keep the sauce warm.

Melt the 10g of butter in a large frying pan. Beat the eggs in a bowl, then add them to the pan and swirl the pan until the base is evenly covered. Pull the edges into the centre as they cook, continuing to swirl so any liquid egg runs to the edges. Leave the omelette to cook over a medium heat until it is almost set – it should have a little wobble.

Pile the fish and sauce on to one half of the omelette and sprinkle with the cheese. Carefully fold the uncovered half of the omelette over the filling and leave it to cook for a couple more minutes until the cheese has melted. Cut the omelette in half and garnish with a few snipped chives.

TORTILLA

Everyone loves this robust Spanish potato omelette. You need a frying pan without a lip, otherwise it's hard to slide the tortilla back into the pan, but if you're worried about turning it you can finish your tortilla off under the grill instead. Good served cold too, so great for picnics.

SERVES 4

olive oil, for frying

1 large Spanish onion, thinly sliced into crescents

300g waxy or salad potatoes, thinly sliced

6 large eggs

sea salt and freshly ground black pepper

Cover the base of a deep, preferably non-stick, lidded frying pan with about 2cm of olive oil. Heat the oil, then add the slices of onion and potato. Sprinkle them with salt, then turn the heat down and partially cover the pan with the lid. Cook, stirring regularly, until the potatoes are done – this can take up to half an hour. If you like, you can parboil the potatoes for 5 minutes first, then proceed as above. Keep a close eye on the potatoes – they should take on as little colour as possible.

Using a slotted spoon, remove the onion and potatoes from the oil and drain them thoroughly on kitchen paper, blotting them if necessary. Put them in a bowl. Tip all but a tablespoon of the oil out of the pan.

Beat the eggs in a bowl and season with salt and pepper, then add the cooked potatoes and onions. Heat the pan with the reserved oil, then pour in the egg, potato and onion mixture, making sure the potatoes and onions are evenly distributed. Cook over a low heat for 8–10 minutes until the egg mixture has set on the bottom and comes away from the base easily when you slide a spatula underneath.

Make sure the top is no longer liquid, then place the frying pan lid or a large flat plate over the pan. Flip the pan over as quickly as you can, so the tortilla drops on to the lid or plate, then slide the tortilla back into the frying pan to continue cooking. Cook for another 3 or 4 minutes until the bottom is just set, then turn out.

Leave the tortilla to cool to room temperature, then cut it into wedges to serve. Great with a tomato salad.

EGGS BENEDICT, ROYALE *and* FLORENTINE

Eggs Benedict is an American brunch dish that several different people claim to have invented. Whoever it was, they did us all a favour. Here's the classic, plus a couple of variations.

SERVES 4

EGGS BENEDICT

4 eggs

2 English muffins

4 slices of ham

a few chives, snipped

EGGS ROYALE

as for Benedict, but using 8 slices smoked salmon instead of ham

EGGS FLORENTINE

as for Benedict, but omit ham and use:

500g fresh spinach

15g butter

grating of nutmeg

squeeze of lemon juice

HOLLANDAISE

50ml white wine vinegar

a few peppercorns

1 bay leaf

1 shallot, finely diced

1 mace blade

3 egg yolks

250g butter, melted

squeeze of lemon juice

pinch of sugar (optional)

salt and black pepper

Poach the eggs (see page 74) but for just 2½ minutes, instead of 3. Carefully place them on kitchen paper to drain.

Now make the hollandaise sauce. Put the vinegar in a small saucepan with 50ml water, the peppercorns, bay leaf, shallot and mace blade. Bring to the boil and simmer until the liquid has reduced to 2 tablespoons. Strain the liquid into a bowl, discard the solids and set aside.

Put the egg yolks in a heatproof bowl with a pinch of salt. Whisk in the vinegar reduction, then set the bowl over a pan of simmering water – the bottom of the pan shouldn't touch the water. Gradually add the melted butter, a few drops at a time to start with, and whisk constantly, until you have a thick emulsion. Continue adding the butter in a slightly faster, steady stream until it is all incorporated and you have a thick, glossy sauce. Taste for seasoning and add a squeeze of lemon juice or a pinch of sugar to balance the flavours. Keep warm.

Split, toast and butter the muffins and put a slice of ham on each half. Bring a large frying pan of water to the boil and add the poached eggs for 30 seconds just to warm them through. Put a poached egg on each muffin half, then spoon over the hollandaise sauce. Sprinkle with chives and serve immediately.

EGGS ROYALE: Follow the method above, but replace the ham with slices of smoked salmon.

EGGS FLORENTINE: Wash the spinach thoroughly, removing any tough stalks. Pile it into a large saucepan and wilt it down over a gentle heat. Drain the spinach thoroughly, squeezing out as much water as you can, then chop. Melt the butter in a frying pan, add the spinach and heat it through. Season with salt and pepper, nutmeg and lemon juice. Divide the spinach between the muffins in place of the ham, then add the eggs and hollandaise as above.

TURKISH EGGS

We first ate this dish in Istanbul and we've loved it ever since. A gorgeous mixture of chilli, yoghurt and poached eggs, it's cropping up more and more in British kitchens now and we reckon this can only be a good thing. Good with warm toasted flatbread.

SERVES 2

300g Greek yoghurt

1 garlic clove, crushed

50g butter

½–1 tsp chilli flakes

1 tsp sweet
smoked paprika

1 tsp white wine
vinegar

4 very fresh eggs

a few parsley leaves,
finely chopped

a few mint leaves,
finely chopped

sea salt and freshly
ground black pepper

Strain the Greek yoghurt if it's particularly liquid, then stir in the garlic and season with salt and pepper. Divide the yoghurt between your serving bowls.

Melt the butter in a small saucepan and add the chilli flakes and smoked paprika. Heat until the butter starts to brown, then remove the pan from the heat and set it aside.

Half fill a saucepan with water, and add the white wine vinegar. Bring the water to the boil, then carefully lower the eggs (still in their shells) into the water and leave them for exactly 20 seconds. Remove the eggs from the water.

Turn the heat down so the water is barely simmering. Carefully crack the eggs into the water and cook them for 3 minutes. Once the eggs are cooked they will rise to the surface. Remove the eggs from the pan and put them on some kitchen paper to drain, then place them on the yoghurt in the bowls.

Drizzle the chilli butter over the eggs and sprinkle some parsley and mint on top. Serve immediately.

MIGAS

There are lots of versions of this traditional Spanish dish – some with scrambled eggs, others with fried. We've gone the scrambled route here and whether you're in Madrid or Macclesfield we hope you enjoy it. Sourdough bread works well and gives plenty of texture.

200g stale bread, cut into cubes

3 tbsp olive oil

150g chorizo, sliced

1 onion, finely chopped

1 red pepper, deseeded and diced

2 garlic cloves, finely chopped

a few sprigs of thyme, leaves finely chopped

6 eggs

50ml whole milk

sea salt and freshly ground black pepper

Put the bread cubes in a bowl, dip your hands in cold water a couple of times and shake the water over the bread. Cover the bread with a damp cloth and leave it to soak for as long as you can – preferably overnight, but for at least 2 hours.

Heat a tablespoon of the oil in a large frying pan. Add the chorizo, and cook until it's well browned on all sides and has given out plenty of oil. Remove the chorizo and set it aside. Add the cubes of bread and fry them for several minutes until they've taken on the colour of the chorizo and crisped up – add a little more oil if necessary. Remove the bread from the frying pan and set it aside. Wipe out the pan with some kitchen paper.

Heat the remaining olive oil in the frying pan and add the onion and red pepper. Cook for a few minutes until they're softening around the edges, then add the garlic. Cook for a further couple of minutes and add the thyme. Beat the eggs lightly with the milk in a bowl and season with salt and pepper. Pour the eggs into the pan and cook quickly until the eggs are set but still soft, stirring constantly. Remove the pan from the heat, then stir in the bread and chorizo. Serve immediately.

SAVOURY EGG CUSTARDS

Custard doesn't always have to be sweet and these little cheesy numbers show the versatility of the humble egg. They are really comforting and delicious and make a nice light lunch or a starter, with some sourdough toast on the side. You'll need four small ramekins, no bigger than 100ml.

SERVES 4

100ml single cream

200ml double cream

1 garlic clove, cut in half

1 sprig of thyme

25g Parmesan cheese, grated

50g Gruyère or similar hard cheese, grated

knob of soft butter, for greasing

2 egg yolks

pinch of cayenne

buttered sourdough toast, to serve

sea salt and white pepper

Pour the creams into a saucepan, add the garlic and thyme, then heat it very gently until the mixture is at blood temperature. Take the pan off the heat and leave the cream to infuse for 10 minutes. Reserve a tablespoon of the Parmesan for sprinkling, then add the rest of the Parmesan and the Gruyère to the cream. Season with salt and a small amount of white pepper and stir the mixture over a very low heat until the cheese has melted. Remove the garlic and sprig of thyme, then leave the mixture to cool completely.

Preheat the oven to 160°C/Fan 140°C/Gas 3. Grease the inside of the ramekins with butter.

Beat the egg yolks into the cream and divide the mixture between the ramekins. Top with a pinch of cayenne and the remaining Parmesan.

Put the ramekins in an ovenproof dish. Add enough just-boiled water to come halfway up the sides of the ramekins, then carefully put the dish into the oven. Cook for about 15 minutes, until the custards are set but they still have a little wobble in the middle.

Allow the custards to cool slightly, then serve with some fingers of buttered sourdough toast.

HUEVOS RANCHEROS

This is a Mexican dish and the name means 'rancher's eggs'. We guess it's meant to set you up for a hard day's work with bucking broncos, but we think it's just right for bikers too!

SERVES 4

4 tortillas

olive oil, for frying

1 or 2 eggs per person

fresh coriander

lime wedges, to serve

SALSA

2 tbsp olive oil

1 small onion, finely chopped

1 red pepper, deseeded and finely chopped

2 garlic cloves, finely chopped

large sprig of thyme

1 tsp dried oregano

2 chipotles in adobo or 2 tbsp chipotle paste

400g can of chopped tomatoes

REFRIED BEANS

1 tbsp olive oil

1 small onion, finely chopped

1 garlic clove, finely chopped

1 bay leaf

½ tsp ground cumin

400g can of pinto beans, drained

sea salt and freshly ground black pepper

First make the salsa. Heat the olive oil in a saucepan, then add the onion and red pepper. Cook them over a low heat until they are very soft and the onion is translucent. This will take at least 10 minutes. Add the garlic, herbs and chipotles or chipotle paste and cook, stirring constantly, for a minute or so.

Pour in the chopped tomatoes with a splash of water and simmer for 20 minutes until reduced a little, then take the pan off the heat. You can purée the salsa if you like, or leave it chunky. Keep the salsa warm.

To make the refried beans, heat the oil in a pan and add the onion. Cook for 5 minutes over a medium heat, then add the garlic, bay leaf and cumin. Stir, then pour in the drained beans. Add 200ml of water, season with salt and pepper, then heat until most of the water has been absorbed. Fish out the bay leaf, then mash the beans roughly so some are whole and others broken up. Turn up the heat again and cook, stirring, until piping hot. The mixture might splutter a bit, so be careful.

Heat a little oil in a large frying pan. Sprinkle a little water over each of the tortillas, then fry them briefly – about 10 seconds on each side – and transfer them to warm plates. Spread some of the refried beans over each tortilla.

Fry the eggs in oil. Add the eggs to the tortillas, then ladle over some of the salsa. Serve immediately, sprinkled with coriander and some lime wedges on the side.

SHAKSHUKA

There are so many recipes for this hugely popular Middle Eastern dish – another savoury egg sensation – and we think it makes a great one-pot lunch or supper as well as a brunch. Here's our latest version, which is packed full of herbs and spices. Give it a try and you'll never look back.

SERVES 4

3 tbsp olive oil

2 large onions, sliced

2 red peppers, deseeded and cut into long slices

2 green peppers, deseeded and cut into long slices

4 garlic cloves, finely chopped

½ tsp cumin seeds

½ tsp caraway seeds

½ tsp cayenne

1 tbsp tomato or red pepper purée

8 ripe tomatoes, cored and chopped, or 2 x 400g cans of tomatoes

1 tsp sugar (optional)

small bunch of coriander, roughly chopped

small bunch of parsley, roughly chopped

8 eggs

8 tbsp thick yoghurt

sea salt and freshly ground black pepper

Heat the olive oil in a large frying pan that has a lid. Add the onions and peppers and season them with salt and pepper. Cook over a medium heat until the veg have softened but still have a little bite – you don't want them to collapse down too much.

Add the garlic and cook for a further 2 minutes, then sprinkle the cumin and caraway seeds and the cayenne into the pan. Stir in the tomato or red pepper purée and cook for a couple more minutes until the paste starts to separate. Add the tomatoes with a splash of water.

Simmer the sauce for about 10 minutes, uncovered, until it has reduced a little. Taste after 5 minutes and add a little sugar if you think the tomatoes need it. Keep an eye on the texture – you don't want the sauce runny, but it mustn't be too dry, either. If it does look dry, add another splash of water. When the sauce is reduced, stir in the herbs.

Make 8 little wells in the sauce. One at a time, break the eggs into a cup and drop them carefully into the wells. Cook for a few more minutes until the whites are just set and the yolks are still runny. You might find it hard to make enough space for 8 eggs in one pan. If so, divide the sauce between 2 pans and cook 4 eggs in each. Serve with some thick yoghurt on the side.

GOAT'S CHEESE *and* CHIVE SOUFFLÉ

Here's one of our favourite soufflés. Don't be scared of soufflés – they are really just a tasty cheese sauce that's enriched with egg yolks and whipped up into a frenzy with the whites, before being popped in the oven to bake. This one will rise like Dave's forehead.

SERVES 4

50g butter, plus extra for greasing

300ml whole milk

1 onion, quartered

1 bay leaf

small bunch of thyme

300g goat's cheese

50g plain flour

4 eggs, separated

3 tbsp finely snipped chives

10g Parmesan, finely grated

sea salt and freshly ground black pepper

Fold a piece of baking parchment in half and tie it around a 13cm soufflé dish. Make sure the paper creates a collar that rises above the dish. Butter the inside of the dish and the paper generously.

Put the milk in a saucepan with the onion, bay leaf and thyme. Bring the milk to a simmer, then remove the pan from the heat and set it aside to infuse for 15 minutes. Preheat the oven to 220°C/Fan 200°C/Gas 7. Place a baking tray in the oven to heat up. Strain the flavoured milk through a fine sieve into a jug. Remove the rind from the goats' cheese and crumble the cheese into small pieces.

Melt the 50g of butter in a saucepan over a low heat. Stir in the flour, cook for a few seconds, then start adding the milk, a little at a time, stirring well in between each addition. When the sauce is smooth and thick, cook for a further 2 minutes, stirring constantly, then remove it from the heat and stir in half the goat's cheese.

Whisk the egg yolks lightly and stir them into the milk, then season to taste. Pour the mixture into a large bowl and cover the surface with cling film to prevent a skin forming. Whisk the egg whites with a pinch of salt until stiff but not dry. They are ready when you can turn the bowl upside down without them sliding out.

Stir the chives into the sauce and add the remaining goat's cheese. Fold in a large spoonful of the egg whites until combined, then fold in the rest. Pour the mixture slowly into the prepared soufflé dish. Sprinkle with the Parmesan and some pepper. Keep the Parmesan towards the centre of the soufflé so it doesn't stick to the paper and stop the soufflé rising.

Bake on the preheated baking tray in the oven for about 25 minutes or until golden brown and risen. Remove the soufflé from the oven, take off the paper and serve immediately.

SMOKED HADDOCK *and* SHRIMP SOUFFLÉS

This is a really tasty recipe. The savoury fish and shrimps work a treat with the robust flavours of the Gruyère and mustard and it's all nicely balanced with the dill. A belter of a dish!

SERVES 6

30g softened butter, plus extra for greasing

2 tbsp finely grated Parmesan cheese

2 tbsp fine dried breadcrumbs

100g smoked haddock fillet (undyed)

2 bay leaves

400ml whole milk

50g brown shrimps

30g plain flour

6 eggs, separated

100g Gruyère cheese, grated

2 tbsp wholegrain mustard

2 tbsp chopped fresh dill

sea salt and freshly ground black pepper

Preheat the oven to 190°C/Fan 170°C/Gas 5 and place a baking sheet in the oven to heat up. Using a pastry brush and making upwards strokes, grease the insides of 6 small ramekins with butter.

Mix the Parmesan and breadcrumbs together and sprinkle them into the buttered dishes, turning each dish on its side and rotating to coat the base and the insides completely. Discard any excess. Pop the dishes in the freezer to chill while you prepare the soufflé mix.

Put the haddock fillet and bay leaves in a saucepan and pour over the milk. Bring the milk to the boil over a low heat, then simmer the milk for 2 minutes. Remove the pan from the heat and lift out the haddock with a slotted spatula. Set the fish aside and pour the milk into a jug. When the haddock is cool enough to handle, remove the skin and any bones and flake the fish into a bowl. Discard the bay leaves. Add the shrimps to the haddock and set aside.

Now make the béchamel sauce. Melt the butter in a heavy-based pan over a medium heat. When the butter has melted, remove the pan from the heat and whisk in the flour until smooth and well combined. Put the pan back on the heat and cook the butter and flour mixture for 2 minutes, whisking continuously. Off the heat, whisk in the milk used to poach the haddock until it's all fully incorporated into the mixture.

Put the pan back on the heat and bring the mixture to the boil, whisking continuously. Reduce the heat and simmer for 3–5 minutes, still whisking, until you have a thick glossy sauce. Take it off the heat, allow it to cool slightly, then stir in the egg yolks, Gruyère, mustard and dill, season with salt and pepper and mix until well combined. Set aside.

In a clean bowl, whisk the egg whites with a pinch of salt until they form soft peaks. Spoon a third of the egg whites into the sauce and beat until the mixture has loosened slightly. Using a metal spoon, gently fold the rest of the whites into the mixture until just combined.

Fold the smoked haddock and shrimp into the soufflé mixture. Fill the dishes with the mixture so that it comes slightly above the top edge. Smooth the surface with a palette knife and then run your finger round the top edge of each ramekin dish to create a small groove around the top. This will help the soufflés to rise evenly.

Place the ramekins on the hot baking sheet and bake them in the oven for about 12 minutes or until well-risen and light golden brown on top but still with a slight wobble. Serve immediately with salad.

BLUE CHEESE *and* SPINACH TWICE-BAKED SOUFFLÉS

As with many things, the rise is never as good the second time around, but these work brilliantly and the twice-cooking method allows you to serve up perfect soufflés for your guests.

SERVES 6

50g butter, plus extra for greasing

200g spinach, well washed

squeeze of lemon juice

1 small onion, finely chopped

40g plain flour

1 tsp English mustard powder

¼ tsp sweet smoked paprika

300ml whole milk

125g blue cheese, crumbled (something not too strong)

4 eggs, separated

chives or parsley (optional)

TO REHEAT

25g Parmesan cheese, grated

180ml double cream

You will need 6 x 150ml ramekins. Grease the ramekins with butter, then line the base of each with a disc of greaseproof paper. Put the spinach in a saucepan (it should still be wet from washing), and squeeze a little lemon juice over it. Wilt the spinach over a medium heat until it has completely collapsed. Drain it thoroughly and squeeze out as much liquid as you can, then chop finely.

Melt the butter in a saucepan. Fry the onion for several minutes until it's soft, then add the flour, mustard powder and paprika. Stir until the flour is fully incorporated. Continue to stir for at least a couple of minutes to cook the flour, then gradually add the milk, stirring constantly, to make a fairly thick béchamel sauce. Stir in the cheese and cook the sauce over a low heat until the cheese has melted. Remove the pan from the heat and leave the sauce to cool. Stir it regularly to stop a skin from forming.

When the mixture is completely cool, beat in the egg yolks, followed by the spinach and the chives or parsley, if using. In a separate bowl, whisk the egg whites to stiff peaks. Fold a couple of tablespoons of the egg whites into the mixture to loosen it a little, then fold in the rest as gently as possible to preserve the volume. Preheat the oven to 200°C/Fan 180°C/Gas 6 and put a baking tray in the oven to heat up.

Spoon the mixture into the ramekins – they should be quite full. Place the ramekins on the tray and cook them in the oven for 15–20 minutes until well risen and golden brown. Remove them and leave to cool. When the soufflés are completely cool, gently remove them from the ramekins and put them in an ovenproof dish. Cover the dish with cling film and pop it in the fridge until needed.

When you want to serve the soufflés, preheat the oven to 200°C/Fan 180°C/Gas 6. Remove the cling film, sprinkle the soufflés with the Parmesan and put a couple of tablespoons of cream on each one. Bake the soufflés for 10 minutes until they're heated through and have puffed up a little more. Serve immediately.

PICKLED EGGS

We do love a pickled egg – an almost forgotten savoury classic – and at one time most pubs would have a jar of them on the bar. They go down a treat with a pint. They're easy to do – just hard boil the eggs, put them in the pickling mixture, then stash them away for a few weeks.

MAKES 6

6 eggs

350ml cider vinegar

1 tbsp salt

1 tbsp sugar

1 tsp chilli flakes or a few dried chillies (optional)

First find a jar that's large enough to hold all 6 eggs – a Kilner jar is ideal. To sterilise it, run it through the hottest setting in your dishwasher, or wash it in plenty of hot, soapy water, then rinse thoroughly. Put it in a low oven (140°C/Fan 120°C/Gas 1) to dry completely.

Bring a saucepan of water to the boil, then gently lower in the eggs. Boil them for 7 minutes exactly, then take the pan off the heat, remove the eggs and run them under cold water to stop them cooking. When they are cool enough to handle, peel them carefully.

Put the cider vinegar in a saucepan with 150ml of water and the salt and sugar. Slowly bring the mixture to the boil, stirring to dissolve the sugar, then simmer for 5 minutes. If using chilli, add it for the last minute.

Pack the eggs into the jar, then pour over the pickling mixture. Seal the jar and leave to cool completely. Leave the eggs for at least 2 weeks before eating, preferably a month, then store the jar in the fridge once opened.

SCOTCH PICKLED EGGS

Like the famous Manchester egg, our recipe began in the pub. In bars in Scotland we saw drinkers take a pickled egg, mash it into a bag of cheese and onion crisps, then wash it down with a pint of heavy. Crazy as it sounds, we've turned this into a culinary keeper. Epic with beer or on a picnic.

MAKES 6

600g Cumberland sausages

2 tbsp celery salt

50g plain flour

100g panko breadcrumbs

1 packet of cheese and onion crisps, crushed

2 eggs

6 pickled eggs (see page 90)

oil, for frying

sea salt and freshly ground black pepper

Remove the sausage meat from the skins and put it all in a bowl. We like Cumberland sausages for their peppery flavour, but you can use anything you fancy, from a herby Lincolnshire to a spicy chorizo. Spread the celery salt on a plate. Spread the flour on a separate plate and season it with salt and pepper. Mix the breadcrumbs with the crisps and put them on another plate, then beat the eggs in a shallow bowl.

Take a pickled egg and roll it in celery salt, then the seasoned flour – the flour helps the sausage meat stick. Make a patty of sausage meat big enough to encase your egg, then wrap it round the egg and form it into a lovely round shape. It helps to have wet hands. Repeat until you've made all your Scotch eggs.

Now dip each sausage-coated egg into the seasoned flour, then the beaten egg and finally roll them in the crisp and crumb mixture.

If you want to deep-fry the eggs, half fill a pan or deep fryer with oil and heat the oil to 160°C. Add the eggs, a few at a time, and cook for about 6 minutes until golden. Alternatively, you can shallow fry the eggs in oil, turning them occasionally until the sausage meat is cooked through and the outsides are golden. Serve up with some good mustard and a few cornichons and onions.

By the way, when we were filming our *Chicken and Egg* telly series we met a brilliant cook called Robert Owen Brown who works in Manchester. He made us his own version of Scotch eggs – Manchester eggs. They were similar to ours but seasoned with smoked paprika and they tasted really amazing.

LEEK, ASPARAGUS *and* GRUYÈRE TART

A tart with a tasty green heart – this combo of leeks, asparagus and cheese works brilliantly and this is delicious hot or cold. You could buy pastry if you like but home-made is so much better.

SERVES 8

1 tbsp olive oil

10g butter

2 leeks, sliced into rounds

200g asparagus, trimmed and cut into short lengths, diagonally

4 eggs

300ml double cream

150g Gruyère cheese, grated

sea salt and freshly ground black pepper

PASTRY

125g cold butter, diced

250g plain flour

50g Parmesan cheese, grated

1 tsp finely chopped thyme leaves

1 egg yolk

To make the pastry, rub the butter into the flour until the mixture has the texture of fine breadcrumbs. Season with salt and add the Parmesan and thyme. Stir in the egg yolk with a knife, then add ice-cold water a teaspoon at a time, cutting it in as you go, until the pastry starts to come together (you will need 1–2 tablespoons of water). Form the pastry into a ball and wrap it in cling film. Chill in the fridge for half an hour.

Roll the pastry out to line a 28cm flan tin. Make sure the pastry is pushed well into the corners, then prick the base all over with a fork. If you have time, put the pastry in the freezer for 10 minutes before baking. Preheat the oven to 200°C/Fan 180°C/Gas 6.

Lay a piece of baking parchment over the pastry and add baking beans. Put the tin on a tray and bake for 15–20 minutes. Remove the beans and parchment and bake the pastry uncovered for a further 5 minutes. Take the tin and baking tray out of the oven and turn the heat down to 180°C/Fan 160°C/Gas 4.

To make the filling, put the olive oil and butter in a frying pan that has a lid. When the butter has melted, add the leeks. Season them with salt and pepper, then add a splash of water. Cover the pan and cook the leeks over a low heat for 10 minutes. Add the asparagus and cook for a further 5 minutes. By now, the vegetables should be glossy and just tender. Take the pan off the heat and set aside to cool.

Break the eggs into a bowl, add the cream and whisk until smooth. Season with salt and pepper. Sprinkle half the cheese over the base of the pastry case, then add the leeks and asparagus. Pour half the egg and cream mixture over the vegetables, then sprinkle the remaining cheese on top. Put the flan tin and baking tray into the oven, then pull the oven shelf out a little so you can pour in the remaining filling. Bake the tart for 35–40 minutes, until the filling is just set with a slight wobble in the centre. Remove the tart from the oven and allow it to cool slightly before serving.

WELSH RAREBIT *with* WELSH ALE

A drop of good Welsh stout is just right for rarebit, or you could use cider, which also works well. Hereford is just over the border from Wales and their cider is great. If you fancy, add a little raw onion to the mixture before grilling. Tasty, tasty, very, very tasty!

— MAKES 6 SLICES —

25g butter

2 tsp plain flour

1 tsp mustard powder

75ml stout

1 tsp Worcestershire sauce

250g Cheddar cheese, grated

3 large egg yolks

6 large slices of granary bread

Melt the butter in a saucepan and whisk in the flour and mustard powder. Cook and stir for a minute or so until the mixture is smooth, then gradually add the stout and the Worcestershire sauce. Bring to the boil and then immediately turn down the heat.

Add the grated cheese and stir until it has melted and the sauce is smooth and fairly liquid. Remove the pan from the heat and set it aside so the sauce can cool a little. Beat in the egg yolks. Preheat your grill to a medium setting.

Toast the bread, then arrange the slices on a rack or baking tray. Drop spoonfuls of the cooled cheese mixture on to the bread, spreading it out almost to the edges. Put the slices under the preheated grill until well browned and slightly puffed up. Serve immediately.

SAVOURY PANCAKES *with* SAUSAGE

Sausage and eggs are an unbeatable combo and this recipe is definitely not just for Pancake Day. Makes a cracking brunch and if you really want to spoil yourself, slather your pancakes with maple syrup.

500g sausage meat

450g self-raising flour

1 tsp baking powder

pinch of salt

3 large eggs, separated

600ml buttermilk

50g butter, melted, plus a little extra

extra butter or lard, for frying

maple syrup, to serve

Put the sausage meat in a frying pan and break it up with a wooden spatula or the edge of a spoon. Fry the meat, stirring regularly and continuing to break it up until it is all well browned and cooked through. If there's a lot of fat in the pan, drain it off, then set the sausage meat aside until needed.

Put the flour in a large bowl with the baking powder and salt. Whisk briefly to combine and remove any lumps, then make a well in the middle. Whisk the egg yolks in a jug with the buttermilk and add the melted butter. Whisk the egg whites in a separate bowl until stiff.

Pour the buttermilk mixture into the flour and whisk until well combined. Add a large spoonful of the egg whites and fold them in with a metal spoon, just to loosen the batter a little. Stir in the rest of the egg whites, keeping as much of the air as possible, to make a fluffy, bubbly batter.

Warm a frying pan (a 20cm pan works well) over a medium heat and brush a little butter or lard over the base. Pour about a ladleful and a half of batter into the pan – it should spread out to cover the base. Sprinkle a couple of tablespoons of the sausage meat over the batter. The pancake will rise up around the sausage as it cooks.

When the pancake has browned on the bottom and is firm enough to flip (when it's cooked more than halfway through), turn it over quickly and cook for another minute on the other side. Turn it out and keep it warm in the oven at a low temperature. Repeat with the rest of the batter and the sausage meat until you've used everything up and you have a lovely pile of pancakes. Serve with a generous puddle of maple syrup.

ROASTS *and* BAKES

CLASSIC ROAST CHICKEN
with sage and onion stuffing

A chicken is everyone's favourite Sunday dinner. There are so many ways of cooking it, but after many decades of practising we find this is the best method and really reliable. We've included two of our favourite stuffings here, so take your pick.

SERVES 4-6

1 x 1.5–1.8kg chicken, giblets removed

25g butter

½ lemon

100ml white wine or vermouth (optional)

sea salt and freshly ground black pepper

SAGE AND ONION STUFFING

15g butter

1 large onion, finely chopped

zest of ½ lemon

5 fresh sage leaves, finely chopped, or 1 tsp dried sage

100g breadcrumbs

1 egg

SAUSAGE MEAT STUFFING

15g butter

1 large onion, finely chopped

200g sausage meat

1 apple, grated

a few sprigs of thyme, finely chopped

If you have time, the day before you roast your chicken, take it out of any packaging, put it on a plate and sprinkle it inside and out with salt. Leave it in the fridge overnight, loosely wrapped in kitchen paper. An hour before you want to start roasting the chicken, remove it from the fridge so it can come up to room temperature.

To make the sage and onion stuffing, melt the butter in a frying pan, add the onion and cook it over a low heat until it's very soft and translucent. Tip the onion into a bowl and let it cool, then add the lemon zest, sage and breadcrumbs. Season well with salt and pepper, then add the egg and mix thoroughly.

If making the sausage meat stuffing, melt the butter and fry the onion as above, then add the sausage meat, apple and herbs.

Preheat the oven to 220°C/Fan 200°C/Gas 7. Weigh the stuffing and add it to the weight of the chicken so you can work out the cooking time. The chicken will need 20 minutes for every 500g, plus 15 minutes at the high temperature to begin with. Fill the cavity of chicken with your chosen stuffing, making sure you leave a little space between the stuffing and the top of the bird, just to let the air circulate. If you have any stuffing left over, put it in the neck end.

Put the chicken in a roasting tin, rub the butter all over it, season, then squeeze the juice from the lemon half over the top. Add the white wine or vermouth along with 100ml of water, or simply use 200ml of water.

Put the chicken in the oven and roast it for 15 minutes. Turn the heat down to 180°C/Fan 160°C/Gas 4 and continue to roast for the time you've worked out. You can test for doneness in a variety of ways. If you have a probe or meat thermometer, the stuffing and the thickest part of the chicken should be 75°C. Or if you pierce the thickest part of the thigh with a skewer, the juices should run clear. The legs should also feel loose when you wiggle them.

1 tbsp flour

100ml white wine

300ml chicken stock

Once the bird is cooked, remove it from the tin and cover it with foil to keep it warm while it rests. Pour the juices from the tin into a jug and strain off any fat, then set the juices aside. To make the gravy, sprinkle the flour into the roasting tin and place the tin over a low heat. Stir the flour into the scrapings at the bottom of the tin to make a roux, then pour in the white wine. Let this bubble up, then gradually add in the defatted pan juices and the chicken stock. At this point you can transfer the gravy to a saucepan if you like – the roasting tin should look clean. Simmer until you have a thin, tasty gravy to serve with the chicken and all the trimmings.

CAULIFLOWER CHEESE

SERVES 4-6

1 large cauliflower, cut into florets

500ml whole milk

2 bay leaves

1 mace blade

a few peppercorns

30g butter

30g plain flour

½ tsp mustard powder

pinch of cayenne

100g Cheddar or Gruyère, grated

sea salt and white pepper

This is cooked in the oven at 180°C/Fan 160°C/Gas 4, so it can go in with the chicken or you can pop it into the hot oven while the chicken is resting.

Bring a large saucepan of water to the boil and add salt. Add the cauliflower and cook it for 4 minutes until it's tender when pierced with a knife. Drain the cauliflower thoroughly and put it in an ovenproof dish.

Pour the milk into a saucepan and add the bay leaves, mace and peppercorns. Place the pan over the heat and bring the milk almost to he boil. Remove the pan from the heat and leave the milk to infuse for a while, or at least until you've made the roux.

Melt the butter in another pan. Add the flour and stir in the mustard powder and cayenne. When you have a smooth roux, keep stirring for a minute or so to cook the flour a little. Strain the milk into a jug and add it to the roux, very gradually to start with and making sure you stir it to a smooth paste with each addition. When the texture is like a liquid sauce, you can add the milk in larger quantities, continuing to stir constantly until it is all incorporated. Add 75g of the cheese and stir until it has melted. Check for seasoning and add salt and pepper, preferably white, if necessary.

Pour the sauce over the cauliflower and sprinkle the rest of the cheese on top. Put the dish in the oven and bake for about 30 minutes until the top is brown and bubbling. Serve with the roast chicken.

LEMONGRASS CHICKEN

This is a wonderfully fragrant, exotic roast. You don't need to make a gravy – just mash the garlic into the pan juices and serve them up. Epic.

SERVES 4-6

1 x 1.5–1.8kg chicken, giblets removed

1 lemongrass stalk

2 Kaffir lime leaves

1 small green chilli, deseeded but left whole

1 lime

small bunch of coriander, very finely chopped

75g butter, softened.

1 garlic bulb, cloves separated but unpeeled

sea salt and freshly ground black pepper

Remove any trussing from the chicken. Bruise or scrunch up the lemongrass – no need to peel it – by hitting it at intervals with the back of a knife or just folding it with your hands. Put it in the cavity of the chicken with the lime leaves and chilli.

Grate the zest of the lime and put it in in a bowl with the coriander and the butter (keep the zested lime for later). Season well with salt and pepper, then mix it all together thoroughly. Starting at the cavity end of the chicken, work the skin away from the breasts and top of the legs of the chicken without tearing it. Spread the butter mixture under the skin, placing it in as an even layer as possible so the breasts and the top of the legs are covered. Tuck any loose skin back under the bird.

Cut the zested lime in half. Season the chicken and squeeze the juice from half the lime over it. Put the other lime half in the chicken. Put the garlic cloves in a roasting tin and place the chicken on top. Roast as on page 104. When the chicken is done, remove it from the oven and place it on a serving platter. Cover it loosely with foil and leave it to rest for 20 minutes. Squish the garlic flesh out of the skins and whisk with the pan juices, then serve these with the chicken.

SI'S BAKED POTATO STUFFED CHICKEN

Spuds and bacon make this a truly British roast and the flavour combination is just right with chicken. Proper comfort food this.

1 medium potato (175–200g)

1 tsp olive oil

2 onions, thickly sliced

1 tsp dried sage

1 tsp dried thyme

1 x 1.5–1.8kg chicken, giblets removed

25g butter

4 slices of streaky bacon

sea salt

Preheat the oven to 200°C/Fan 180°C/Gas 6. Pierce the potato all over with a fork and score a cross in it. Rub the potato with olive oil and then season it with salt. Wrap it in foil and bake in the oven for about an hour.

Arrange the onions over the base of a roasting tin and sprinkle over the sage and thyme. Place the chicken on top. Squish the baked potato to break it up a bit, then season it with more salt and pepper and stuff it inside the chicken. Rub the butter over the chicken and season with salt. Stretch out the bacon slices, then cut them in half and place them over the chicken breast and the top of the legs.

Put the chicken in the oven and roast as on page 104. While the chicken is resting, remove the onions from the tin. Skim off as much of the fat as you can and serve the pan juices as they are or make gravy as on page 105.

ROAST CHICKEN
with herb and couscous stuffing

Here's a roast chicken with a touch of the Middle East. Pop some couscous stuffing inside and brush the chicken with a pomegranate molasses glaze and you have something extra special for Sunday lunch.

SERVES 4-6

1 x 1.5–1.8kg chicken, giblets removed

1 tbsp pomegranate molasses

1 tbsp olive oil

juice of ½ lemon, plus an extra squeeze for serving

¼ tsp cinnamon

¼ tsp cayenne

sea salt and freshly ground black pepper

HERB AND COUSCOUS STUFFING

50g couscous

small bunch of coriander, finely chopped

small bunch of mint, finely chopped

1 garlic clove, crushed

25g dried sour cherries or apricots, finely chopped

20g pistachios or almonds, chopped

zest of 1 lemon

¼ tsp cinnamon

1 tbsp olive oil

First make the stuffing. Put the couscous in a bowl and season it with salt and pepper. Pour over 75ml of tepid water and leave to stand until the liquid has completely absorbed and the couscous is tender. Add all the remaining ingredients to the couscous and mix together thoroughly. The mixture will be crumbly, so spoon it into the cavity of the chicken rather than trying to clump it together with your hands.

Put the chicken in a roasting tin. Mix the pomegranate molasses, oil, lemon juice and spices in a bowl to make a glaze and season with salt and pepper. Brush the chicken lightly with the glaze – don't use all of it. Put the chicken in the oven and cook as on page 104. Brush the chicken with more glaze once it has been cooking for half an hour and again after 45 minutes. Drop a little glaze on to any exposed stuffing too.

When the chicken is cooked, rest it as before and add a squeeze of lemon juice to any liquid remaining in the tin to make a gravy.

MEDITERRANEAN ROAST CHICKEN

Roast chicken goes on holiday in this recipe, with flavours of the Mediterranean such as olives, capers, herbs and lemon. And the whole thing is topped up with a beautiful tomatoey gravy. This is just the thing for a summer treat.

SERVES 4-6

1 x 1.5–1.8kg chicken, giblets removed

a few sprigs of thyme

a few sprigs of rosemary

1 strip of thinly pared lemon zest

olive oil

juice of 1 lemon

100ml white wine

200g ripe tomatoes, roughly chopped

sea salt and freshly ground black pepper

MEDITERRANEAN STUFFING

2 tbsp olive oil

75g ciabatta loaf, torn or chopped into cubes

1 small onion, finely chopped

50g black olives, pitted and finely sliced

25g capers

1 garlic clove, chopped

1 tsp dried mixed herbs

4 tbsp finely chopped parsley

handful of basil leaves, finely chopped

First make the stuffing. Heat the olive oil in a large frying pan. Add the cubes of ciabatta and season them with salt and pepper. Fry over a high heat, stirring constantly, until the bread is crisp and well browned. Remove the pan from the heat and tip the bread into a bowl. Add all the remaining stuffing ingredients and stir well, then spoon the stuffing into the cavity of the chicken.

Put the herbs and lemon peel in a roasting tin and place the chicken on top. Drizzle the chicken with the olive oil and rub it in, then season with salt and pepper and squeeze over the lemon juice. Roast the chicken as on page 104.

Remove the chicken from the oven and transfer it to a board or platter. Cover with foil and leave to rest for 20 minutes. Strain off all the liquid from the roasting tin and spoon away the fat. Set the roasting tin over a high heat and deglaze with the white wine, making sure you scrape up any brown bits from the bottom of the tin and allow them to dissolve into the liquid. When the wine is well reduced, add the tomatoes. Simmer them for just a few minutes so they burst away from their skins, then add some of the strained cooking liquid. Serve this gravy with the chicken.

BEER CAN CHICKEN

This might look like a funny way of cooking a chicken but the steam rising from the beer keeps the meat lovely and juicy as it cooks. Use a beer can or one of those vertical roasters you can now buy, which are steadier and easier to cope with. You can use cider instead of beer if you like. A great recipe for a barbecue party. Cheers!

SERVES 4-6

1 x 1.8kg chicken, giblets removed

1 tbsp sweet smoked paprika

1 tbsp mustard powder

½ tsp cayenne

1 tsp garlic powder

1 tsp dried oregano

1 tbsp light soft brown sugar or honey

zest of 1 lemon

50g butter, softened

440ml can of beer

lemon wedges, to serve

sea salt and freshly ground black pepper

Prepare your barbecue or preheat your oven to its highest setting.

Season the inside of the chicken with salt. Mix together the paprika, mustard powder, cayenne, garlic powder, oregano, sugar or honey and the lemon zest with lots of black pepper and a teaspoon of salt in a small bowl. Add the butter and knead it all together, then rub the whole lot over the chicken, making sure every bit of skin is covered.

Pour out half the beer from the can – up to you what you do with it! Sit the chicken over the can and place it on a roasting tin. If roasting your bird in the oven, cook it for 15 minutes at the highest temperature, then turn the oven down to 200°C/Fan 180°C/Gas 6 and roast for a further 45-60 minutes. Check that the chicken is cooked through, then cover it with foil and leave it to rest for 20 minutes before serving.

If you are cooking your chicken on a barbecue, make sure the coals are very hot. If you have a grid small enough to place directly on top of or just very slightly above the coals, use this and put the roasting tin on top. Otherwise, put the roasting tin directly on to the coals, making it as stable as possible, and put the lid on the barbecue. Roast the chicken for an hour and 20 minutes, checking the coals regularly, until it is cooked through. Remove the chicken from the barbecue, then cover it with foil and leave it to rest for 20 minutes.

Serve with lemon wedges – the juice really enhances the fantastic flavour of the chicken.

SPATCHCOCKED CHICKEN

Spatchcocking a chicken simply means flattening it so it cooks in a shorter time than usual. The beauty of spatchcocking is that the meat cooks quickly and evenly and every bit of skin gets good and crispy. Quick joke: why did the chicken cross the road? To see his flat-mate!

SERVES 4-6

1 x 1.5–1.8kg chicken

1 tsp salt

1 tsp black peppercorns

1 tsp dried herbs

1 tsp sweet smoked paprika

zest and juice of 1 lemon

2 tbsp olive oil

200ml vermouth or white wine

To spatchcock the chicken, turn it breast-side down with the legs towards you. Using very sturdy kitchen scissors or poultry shears, cut down one side of the parson's nose and the backbone. Then turn the chicken around and cut along the other side of the backbone, back to the parson's nose. Remove this piece and put it aside to use for stock.

Flip the chicken breast-side up again and press firmly down on the breast bone to flatten it out a little. See page 370 for more on spatchcocking.

Mix the salt, peppercorns, herbs, paprika and lemon zest in a small bowl, then whisk in the oil. Rub this mixture all over the chicken, then put it in a bowl or a plastic bag and pour over the lemon juice. Leave the chicken to marinate for at least an hour or as long as overnight in the fridge. Be sure to take it out of the fridge an hour before you want to cook it.

Preheat the oven to its highest setting. Pour the vermouth or white wine into a roasting tin and place the chicken on a rack set above it. Put the tin in the oven and turn the temperature down to 200°C/Fan 180°C/Gas 6. Roast for 35-40 minutes until the skin is crisp and the chicken is cooked through. To test, put a thermometer into the thickest part of the leg – it should read 75°C. Alternatively, simply insert a skewer for a couple of seconds – if it's too hot to place on the inside of your wrist comfortably, the chicken is done.

Serve the chicken with the pan juices poured over the top.

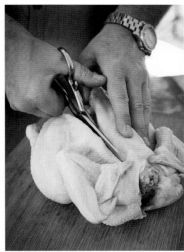

SI'S POT ROAST

Lovely flavours in here – onions, orange and garlic – and the aniseedy tang of the celeriac works so well with the citrus. This is the ultimate one-pot wonder and guaranteed not to be dry.

SERVES 4-6

1 tbsp olive oil

15g butter

12 small onions or shallots, peeled

200g celeriac, cut into large chunks

2 carrots, cut into chunks

1 garlic bulb, separated into cloves, unpeeled

1 x 1.5kg chicken

¼ orange

bouquet garni made up of 1 sprig of parsley, 1 sprig of oregano and a bay leaf

100ml white wine

150ml orange juice (preferably freshly squeezed)

250ml chicken stock

sea salt and freshly ground black pepper

Preheat the oven to 200°C/Fan 180°C/Gas 6. Heat the olive oil and butter in a large flameproof casserole dish. Add the onions or shallots, the celeriac and carrots and cook them over a medium-high heat until everything is well browned. Remove the vegetables from the casserole dish with a slotted spoon and set them aside.

Pierce half the garlic cloves with a knife and put them in the chicken cavity along with the piece of orange. Put the chicken in the casserole dish and brown it well on all sides, then turn it breast-side up. Add the rest of the garlic and the bouquet garni, then arrange the browned vegetables around the chicken. Season everything with salt and pepper.

Pour over the white wine and bring it to the boil. Let it bubble for a couple of minutes, then add the orange juice and chicken stock. Bring it all back to the boil, then put a lid on the casserole dish, put it in the oven and cook the chicken for 45 minutes. Take the lid off and cook for another 15 minutes so the chicken can brown.

Check the chicken is cooked through – the juices should run clear and the legs should be loose. If you have a meat thermometer check that the internal temperature is 75°C. Remove the chicken and vegetables from the casserole dish and arrange them on a platter. Cover them loosely with foil to keep warm while the chicken rests and you prepare the gravy.

Squash the garlic flesh out of the skins and mash them into the cooking juices. Put the casserole dish back on the hob and bring the juices to the boil, then continue to cook until the liquid is reduced by about half and you have a fairly thin but creamy-looking gravy. Strain the gravy into a jug and serve it with the scrumptious chicken and vegetables.

CHICKEN *with* 40 CLOVES *of* GARLIC

The best part of this dish is the garlic which is cooked until it's meltingly soft. It has an amazing flavour and because it's cooked for such a long time it's quite mild too. This is a belter of a recipe and great served with some spring greens and colcannon.

SERVES 4-6

250g shallots (small ones, not banana shallots)

1 x 1.5kg chicken, giblets removed

½ lemon, halved

1 bay leaf

25g butter

1 tbsp olive oil

1 tbsp finely chopped fresh thyme

40 garlic cloves, unpeeled

150ml vermouth

250ml chicken stock

2 tbsp chopped fresh tarragon leaves

100ml double cream or crème fraiche

sea salt and freshly ground black pepper

Preheat the oven to 200°C/Fan 180°C/Gas 6. Place the shallots in a bowl, cover them with just-boiled water and leave them to stand for about 5 minutes. This will make the skins easier to remove. Remove any string from the chicken and place the lemon and bay leaf in the cavity. Season the chicken inside and out with plenty of salt and black pepper.

Melt the butter with the oil in a large flameproof casserole dish. Brown the chicken for a couple of minutes on each side, then sprinkle it with the chopped thyme. Drain the shallots and, once they are cool enough to handle, peel off the skin, halving any larger ones. Add the shallots and the garlic cloves to the casserole, nestling them around the chicken.

Pour over the vermouth and chicken stock and bring the liquid to a simmer on the hob. Cover the casserole dish with a tight-fitting lid, then transfer it to the oven. Bake for 1 hour and 15 minutes, or until the chicken is cooked and the garlic is completely softened.

Transfer the chicken, garlic and shallots to a warm dish and cover it with foil and a couple of dry tea towels. Tilt the casserole dish to one side and skim off any fat from the surface of the cooking juices and discard it.

Put the casserole dish back on the hob and stir in the tarragon and cream or crème fraiche into the cooking juices. Bring to a gentle simmer, while stirring, and cook for about 3 minutes. Season the sauce to taste, then pour it into a warm jug. Serve the chicken with the sauce and have some crusty bread on the side so you can squeeze the garlic out of its skin and spread it on the bread. Outrageously good.

CHICKEN CORDON BLEU

These stuffed chicken breasts look good and fancy to impress your friends but they're not hard to cook and most of the preparation can be done in advance. If you love chicken kiev, you will love these too – a 70s classic brought nicely up to date.

4 skinless, boneless chicken breasts

4 thin slices smoked ham (about 130g)

60g Emmental cheese, cut into 4 pieces

8 tsp cranberry sauce

25g plain flour

200g breadcrumbs

2 eggs

5 tbsp vegetable oil

sea salt and freshly ground black pepper

Using a sharp knife, remove the mini-fillet from each breast and set them aside. Butterfly the chicken breasts (see page 368).

Take a chicken breast and its mini-fillet and place it between 2 sheets of cling film, then bash it with a rolling pin until it is about 5mm thick all over. Remove the top layer of cling film and cover the flattened breast with a slice of ham. Place a chunk of cheese in the middle of the ham and top it with 2 teaspoons of the cranberry sauce.

Put the flattened mini-fillet of chicken over the fillings and then carefully wrap up the breast by bringing the pointy end over the cheese so it's tucked neatly inside. Then, using the bottom layer of cling film, roll the breast up tightly to make a parcel. Make sure the cling film stays on the outside so you can remove it afterwards. Repeat with the remaining chicken breasts.

Sprinkle the flour over a large plate and season it with salt and pepper. Scatter 50g of the breadcrumbs on another large plate. Whisk the eggs in a shallow bowl.

Dust one of the stuffed breasts thoroughly in flour and pat it lightly to remove any excess. Roll the floured chicken in the egg, then coat it in the breadcrumbs. Dip the chicken back in the egg and then coat it in the crumbs again. Repeat with the remaining chicken breasts, adding 50g of the breadcrumbs to the plate for each breast so they don't get too sticky.

Preheat the oven to 220°C/Fan 200°C/Gas 7. Heat the oil in a large frying pan and fry the breasts over a medium heat for 1 or 2 minutes on all sides, or until golden brown. Put the browned breasts on a baking tray and cook them in the oven for 25 minutes, or until the chicken is cooked through. Serve at once while they're piping hot.

CITRUS-MARINATED CHICKEN THIGHS

Fennel goes well with chicken and the tang of orange and lemon really brings out all the flavours in this tray bake. This is a beautifully fresh and tasty supper that we think you're going to love.

--------- SERVES 4 ---------

8 chicken thighs or drumsticks or 4 chicken legs, skin on and bone in

1 tbsp olive oil, plus extra for drizzling

juice and zest of 1 lemon

juice of 1 orange

2 garlic cloves, crushed or grated

1 tbsp chopped fresh oregano

2 fennel bulbs, cut into wedges

half a garlic bulb, separated into cloves, unpeeled

2–3 strips of thinly pared orange zest

150ml white wine

50g black olives

a few sprigs of oregano, mint and fennel to garnish

sea salt and freshly ground black pepper

Put the chicken in a bowl or a large plastic bag and season it with salt and pepper. Mix the olive oil, lemon juice and zest, orange juice, crushed or grated garlic and the oregano in a jug to make the marinade, then pour it over the chicken. Leave the chicken to marinate for at least an hour, but preferably for several hours or overnight in the fridge.

If the chicken has been in the fridge, take it out an hour before you want to cook to allow it to come up to room temperature. Preheat the oven to 200°C/Fan 180°C/Gas 6.

Arrange the wedges of fennel in a roasting tin (save some of the fronds to use as a garnish) and sprinkle over the garlic cloves and pared orange zest. Place the chicken pieces on top of the fennel, then pour over any remaining marinade. Mix the wine with 50ml of water and pour it around the chicken (not over it), then drizzle with a little more olive oil.

Bake the chicken in the oven for about an hour, until the fennel is tender and slightly coloured around the edges and the chicken is cooked through with a good crisp skin. Sprinkle in the black olives and garnish with plenty of herbs. Serve the chicken and fennel with the delicious juices from the roasting tin.

CHICKEN *and* SAUSAGE TRAY BAKE

Packed with veg as well as chunky sausages, this is a great one-pot dish and as you all know we're big fans of one-pot wonders. It's quick as anything to put together and all you need is a nice pile of greens on the side.

4 chicken thighs, skin on and bone in

4–6 meaty pork sausages

500g piece of pumpkin or squash, cut into wedges

2 onions, cut into wedges

a few sprigs of thyme, or 1 tsp dried thyme

1 tbsp olive oil

50ml red wine

1 tbsp maple syrup

1 tsp red wine vinegar

½ tsp chilli flakes (optional)

200g chestnut mushrooms, halved

sea salt and freshly ground black pepper

Preheat the oven to 220°C/Fan 200°C/Gas 7.

Put the chicken thighs skin-side up in a roasting tin with the sausages, pumpkin or squash and the onions and season them with salt and pepper. Sprinkle the thyme over everything and drizzle over the olive oil. Mix the red wine with 100ml of water and pour it into the tin, then put the tray bake in the oven to roast for 30 minutes.

Take the tin out and turn the sausages over so that they can brown all over. Mix the maple syrup with the red wine vinegar and spoon it over the contents of the roasting tin. Sprinkle over the chilli flakes, if using, then add the mushrooms and drizzle with a little more olive oil.

Roast for a further 25-30 minutes until everything is cooked through and well browned.

Serve the chicken, sausages and veg with any pan juices spooned over them and a good pile of greens.

CHICKEN PARMIGIANA

This is our take on the Italian baked aubergine dish, made even more delicious with breadcrumbed chicken. Us northerners have another version too, known as Parmo – the signature dish of Middlesbrough! You fry the chicken as below, slather it with béchamel sauce, then top with lots of grated cheese and put it under the grill to brown.

SERVES 4

4 skinless, boneless chicken breasts

75g Parmesan cheese, grated

75g breadcrumbs

1 tsp dried oregano

a few basil leaves, finely chopped

100g plain flour

2 eggs

sea salt and freshly ground black pepper

TOMATO SAUCE

1 tbsp olive oil

1 onion, finely chopped

2 garlic cloves, finely chopped

100ml red wine

1 tsp dried oregano

400g can of tomatoes

pinch of sugar (optional)

TO ASSEMBLE

garlic clove

2 balls of mozzarella, sliced

handful of basil leaves, to serve

To make the sauce, heat the oil in a saucepan and add the onion. Fry it gently until it's soft and translucent, then add the garlic. Cook for a further couple of minutes, then add the red wine. Allow it to bubble fiercely until reduced by half, then add the oregano and tomatoes and season with salt and pepper. Cover the pan and simmer the sauce for 10 minutes, then remove the lid. Taste and add a pinch of sugar if you think the tomatoes aren't sweet enough. Simmer for a further 10 minutes, uncovered, until you have a well-reduced sauce; you don't want anything too wet for this dish as it will make the chicken soggy.

Preheat the oven to 200°C/Fan 180°C/Gas 6. Butterfly the chicken (see page 368), then put the breasts between 2 sheets of cling film and flatten them slightly with a rolling pin. Season the chicken with salt and pepper. Mix the Parmesan with the breadcrumbs, oregano and basil. Put half the flour on one plate and season it with salt and pepper. Beat one of the eggs in a bowl and spread half the Parmesan mixture on another plate.

Dip a chicken breast in the flour, then dust off any excess and dip into the egg. Finally coat it in the breadcrumbs and Parmesan, pressing the mixture firmly on to the chicken. Repeat with the second chicken breast. When you have used up this first lot of coatings, add the rest, on clean plates if necessary, and coat the remaining chicken breasts. Arrange the chicken breasts on a baking tray and drizzle them with a little oil, then bake them in the oven for 12-15 minutes until just cooked through. Remove the chicken but leave the oven on.

To assemble, take a large, shallow oven dish that will take all the chicken in a single layer. Cut the garlic clove in half and rub it over the dish. Spread the sauce over the base of the dish, then place the chicken on top. Arrange the mozzarella over the chicken so it is almost completely covered. Bake in the oven for 15-20 minutes until everything is piping hot and the mozzarella is melted and browned. Garnish with a few basil leaves before serving.

LOCKHART SMOKED CHICKEN
and devilled eggs

They love their barbecue in the US, and the Lockhart Smokehouse in Texas does the real McCoy. We went there when filming the US episode of our 'Chicken and Egg' series and were knocked out by the food. It's hard to replicate exactly at home, but they were kind enough to give us their recipe and we've adapted it for use with a home barbecue. Try the devilled eggs too. Wow!

——————————— SERVES 4 ———————————

1 x 1.5kg chicken

RUB

2 tbsp fine sea salt

1 tbsp dark brown sugar

1 tbsp ground black pepper

1 tsp hot smoked paprika

1 tsp ground cumin

2 garlic cloves, crushed

1 tbsp olive oil

FOR THE BARBECUE

2 foil takeaway trays, one half-filled with water.

lumpwood charcoal

2 large handfuls of wood chips, soaked for 15 minutes in water then drained

Start the day before you want to cook the chicken. Mix together the rub ingredients in a bowl and spread half the mixture over the chicken. Cover the chicken or put it in a plastic bag and leave it in the fridge overnight. Reserve the remaining rub mixture.

The following day, prepare your barbecue. Place the empty foil tray on one half of the barbecue base (this will act as your drip tray) and light the charcoal on the other side of the barbecue. The drip-tray 'cool' side will be used for smoking your chicken. When the coals are white hot and no flame is visible, sprinkle the drained wood chips on top. Place the grill over the top of your coals, close the lid of the barbecue and leave it to heat up for 15 minutes. If you have a thermometer, measure the temperature – it's ready when it reaches 200°C.

Meanwhile, finish preparing the chicken. Pat it dry and remove any excess rub. Take the reserved rub mixture and spread it all over the chicken.

Place the water-filled foil tray over the hot coals (this helps to regulate the temperature) and place the chicken on the opposite 'cool' side, over the drip tray. Put the lid back on the barbecue and make sure the smoke vent is open and over the 'cool' side. This will encourage the smoke to flow around the chicken. Leave for 2-3 hours, checking every hour and adding more charcoal, soaked wood chips or water if necessary. The chicken is ready when the juices run clear from the thickest part of the thigh. When the chicken is cooked, leave it to rest for 20 minutes before serving.

DEVILLED EGGS

MAKES 12

12 large eggs

85ml mayonnaise, plus
an extra tbsp (optional)

3 tsp Dijon mustard

1 tsp sriracha or hot
sauce

45g finely chopped
smoked chicken

½ small red onion,
finely chopped

salt, to taste

smoked paprika or
cayenne pepper

Bring a large pan of water to the boil and boil the eggs for 10 minutes exactly. Cool them under running water and peel. Cut the peeled eggs in half then scoop out the yolks into a bowl with a teaspoon.

In a blender, whizz together the mayonnaise, mustard, sriracha or hot sauce, smoked chicken, red onion and a little salt to taste. Add the egg yolks and blend again. If the mixture is too dry, add another tablespoon of mayonnaise to loosen it. Spoon a generous amount of the filling back into the halved egg whites and sprinkle over some smoked paprika or cayenne.

These are great just as they are, but if you've been smoking your chicken, just pop the eggs in for 3 minutes for an even smokier flavour.

PIES and PUDDINGS

CHICKEN, HAM *and* LEEK PIE

We think this has to be our last supper pie – it's that good and we just had to include it here in our chicken book. You can use shop-bought pastry if you like, but for the very best eating experience, make your own using our fab pastry recipe on page 360.

SERVES 6

450ml chicken stock

3 skinless, boneless chicken breasts

75g butter

2 leeks, trimmed and cut into 1cm slices

2 garlic cloves, crushed

50g plain flour

200ml whole milk

2–3 tbsp white wine (optional)

150ml double cream

150g thickly sliced ham, cut into 2cm chunks

sea salt and freshly ground black pepper

PASTRY

500g shortcrust pastry (shop-bought or make your own – see page 360)

flour, for dusting

beaten egg, to glaze

Heat the stock in a saucepan. Add the chicken and bring the stock to a low simmer, then cover the pan and cook for 10 minutes. Remove the breasts and set them aside, then pour the stock into a jug for later.

Melt 25g of the butter in a large saucepan. Stir in the leeks and fry them gently for 2 minutes, stirring occasionally, until just softened, then add the garlic and cook for a further minute. Add the remaining butter and stir in the flour once it's melted. Cook for 30 seconds, stirring constantly.

Slowly pour the milk into the pan, a little at a time, stirring well. Gradually add 250ml of the stock and then the wine, if using, and stir until the sauce is smooth and thickened slightly. Bring to a gentle simmer and cook for 3 minutes. Season the sauce to taste, then remove the pan from the heat and stir in the cream. Pour the sauce into a large bowl and cover the surface with cling film to prevent a skin forming. Set aside to cool.

Preheat the oven to 200°C/Fan 180°C /Gas 6. Put a baking tray in the oven to heat up.

Cut off about a third of the pastry for the lid of the pie. Roll out the remaining pastry on a lightly floured surface until it's about 5mm thick and 4cm larger than the pie dish. Lift the pastry over the rolling pin and place it gently into the pie dish. Press the pastry firmly up the inside of the dish and leave the excess pastry overhanging the sides. Cut the chicken breasts into bite-sized pieces and stir them and the ham and leeks into the sauce. Pour all the filling into the pie dish.

Roll out the rest of the pastry and brush the rim of the dish with beaten egg. Cover the pie with the pastry lid and press the edges together firmly to seal. Trim away any excess pastry. Make a small hole in the centre of the pie with the tip of a knife and glaze the top of the pie with beaten egg. Put the dish on the preheated tray in the oven and bake for 35-40 minutes until golden brown on top and piping hot inside.

CHICKEN CASSEROLE *with* POTATO COBBLER

This is brilliant and not just a load of old cobblers. A cobbler is a sort of pie, but instead of having a pastry top it's covered with 'cobbles' made from a scone-like mixture. They're really easy to prepare and our potato version is a perfect match for this tasty chicken and mushroom filling.

SERVES 4

8 skinless, boneless chicken thighs

3 tbsp vegetable oil

4 rashers of streaky bacon, cut into strips

2 onions, sliced

2 celery sticks, thinly sliced

150g button mushrooms, wiped and quartered

400g can chopped tomatoes

600ml chicken stock

1 bay leaf

2 tsp dried thyme

375g carrots, sliced

1 tbsp cornflour

2 leeks, sliced

sea salt and freshly ground black pepper

COBBLER TOPPING

350g floury potatoes, such as King Edwards or Maris Pipers

250g self-raising flour, plus extra for dusting

1 tsp fine sea salt

100g cold butter, cut into cubes

125ml whole milk, plus extra for brushing

First make the mash for the cobbler topping. Peel the potatoes and cook them until tender, then drain, mash and leave them to cool.

Cut each chicken thigh into 4 pieces and season them with salt and pepper. Heat the oil in a large frying pan and fry the chicken until lightly browned all over. It's best to do this in a couple of batches so you don't overcrowd the pan. Put the browned chicken in a flameproof casserole dish. Preheat the oven to 200°C/Fan 180°C/Gas 6.

Put the bacon, onions and celery in the frying pan and fry for 4 or 5 minutes until lightly browned, stirring often. Add the mushrooms and cook for another minute. Tip everything into the casserole dish with the chicken, then stir in the tomatoes, stock, bay leaf, thyme and carrots. Bring everything to a simmer on the hob, then cover the dish loosely with a lid and put it in the oven for 30 minutes.

While the chicken is cooking, finish making the topping. Put the flour and salt in a bowl and rub in the butter with your fingertips until the mixture resembles breadcrumbs. Add 250g of mash – you can use up any leftovers in another recipe – and rub it together with the butter and flour. Stir in the milk and mix to form a soft dough. Turn the dough out on to a floured surface and roll it into a thick sausage, about 24cm long. Cut this into 12 rounds, each about 2cm thick.

Take the chicken out of the oven and check the seasoning, adding more if needed. Mix the cornflour with 2 tablespoons of water and stir this into the casserole, then add the leeks.

Top the chicken with the potato 'cobbles', overlapping them slightly, so they almost cover the filling. Brush them with milk to glaze and season with salt and pepper. Put the dish back in the oven without the lid for another 30 minutes, or until the cobbler topping is well risen and golden brown. Serve immediately.

CHICKEN *and* MUSHROOM PIE *with puff pastry*

We've made this a double-crust pie because we do love our pastry, but if you prefer you can just pop on a puff lid – you'll need about a third of the amount of pastry listed here – and it will still be fab. A winner of a pie, and chicken and mushrooms are almost as classy a pairing as we are.

SERVES 4

25g plain flour, plus extra for dusting

500g block of all-butter puff pastry

1 tbsp olive oil

35g butter

600g skinless, boneless chicken thighs, diced (or breasts if you prefer)

1 small onion, finely chopped

250g button or chestnut mushrooms, wiped and sliced

75ml white wine

250ml chicken stock

50ml double cream (optional)

leaves from a sprig of thyme

2 tbsp finely chopped parsley

1 small sprig of tarragon, finely chopped (optional)

beaten egg, to glaze

sea salt and freshly ground black pepper

Dust your work surface with flour and roll out half the pastry. Use it to line a 750ml pie dish. Leave the pastry slightly overhanging the rim of the dish and put it in the fridge to chill.

Heat the olive oil and 10g of the butter in a large frying pan. When the butter has melted, add the chicken and season it with salt and pepper. Cook the chicken over a medium-high heat until it is seared on all sides – this shouldn't take more than 2 minutes.

Remove the chicken from the frying pan with a slotted spoon, then add the onion and mushrooms. Cook over a medium heat until everything is glossy and well softened, then remove it all from the pan and set aside. Add the white wine to the pan and let it bubble for a minute, stirring up all the sticky bits from the bottom of the pan, then pour it into a jug.

Heat the remaining butter in a saucepan. Add the 25g of flour and stir for at least 2-3 minutes to cook out the raw flavour of the flour. Gradually add the wine, followed by the stock, until you have a smooth béchamel sauce. Add the cream, if using, and simmer for another couple of minutes. Stir in the chicken, onion, mushrooms and all the herbs, then leave to cool.

Preheat the oven to 200°C/Fan 180°C/Gas 6. Transfer the cooled chicken mixture to the pie dish. Roll out the remaining pastry to fit the dish and if you have enough left over, cut thin strips to build up the rim a little first. Cover with the pastry lid, sealing the edges with cold water.

Cut a couple of slits in the pie, then brush the top with the beaten egg. Bake the pie in the oven for 40-45 minutes until the pastry is a deep golden brown and well puffed up, and the filling is piping hot.

CHICKEN *and* LEEK PUDDING
with sage suet crust

Our mams both used to make suet puddings and we still love them – a real guilty pleasure, like Dave loving Abba! The sage suet crust when mixed with the cooking juices is sublime and we like the touch of mustard in the crust for extra oomph. If you're not a mustard fan, leave it out.

SERVES 4

500g diced chicken
(a mixture of skinless,
boneless thighs
and breasts)

zest of 1 lemon

a few crushed white
peppercorns

a few fresh sage leaves

100ml white wine
or vermouth

250g leeks, trimmed
and sliced into
2cm rounds

1 tbsp plain flour

½ tsp mustard powder

150ml chicken stock

sea salt

SUET CRUST

225g self-raising flour

1 tsp baking powder

1 tsp dried sage

½ tsp mustard powder

100g suet

100–150ml milk

butter, for greasing

First, put the chicken in a bowl and add the lemon zest, peppercorns and sage leaves. Pour over the wine and leave the chicken to marinate for at least an hour or overnight in the fridge.

To make the suet crust, put the flour, baking powder, sage and mustard powder in a bowl. Stir, add the suet and rub it into the flour until the mixture resembles breadcrumbs. Gradually add the milk, cutting it in with a knife until the mixture comes together as a soft but not sticky dough.

Roll the dough out into a large round and cut out a quarter to a third of it to make the lid. Grease a 1.2-litre pudding bowl and line it with the pastry, making sure the sides are covered and the joins are well sealed.

Mix the leeks with the chicken. Mix the flour with the mustard powder in a small bowl and season with salt. Pour this over the chicken and mix everything well with your hands or a metal spoon. Pack it all into the suet crust, then slowly pour in as much of the stock as you can.

Make a round lid with the remaining dough and place it on top of the filling. Press the edges together until you are sure the pudding is well sealed. Cut a circle of baking paper to fit over the basin and butter it liberally, then make a pleat in the middle. Cover the pudding with the paper, then a piece of foil, again with a pleat in the middle. Secure the foil with string or a sturdy rubber band.

Put the pudding in a steamer over a large saucepan or if you don't have a steamer, fold up a tea towel, put it in the pan and place the pudding on top. Add boiling water to about halfway up the sides of the basin and put a lid on the pan. Steam for about 2 hours, making sure you check on the water levels regularly. Always top up with boiling water.

When you are ready to serve, remove the foil and run a palette knife round the rim of the pudding. Turn it out on to a plate and serve at once with the potato croquettes.

POTATO CROQUETTES

You can add some herbs to these if you like or leave them plain. They make a cracking side dish with the pud – or just with some grilled chicken and salad.

750g potatoes, peeled and cut into chunks

25g butter

2 egg yolks

50g Cheddar or Parmesan cheese, grated

50g flour

75g panko breadcrumbs

1 egg

vegetable oil, for drizzling or frying

sea salt and freshly ground black pepper

Put the potatoes in a saucepan, cover them with water and add salt. Bring to the boil, then turn down to simmer until the potatoes are tender when pierced with the point of a knife – this should take about 15 minutes.

Drain the potatoes well and mash them thoroughly, preferably with a ricer. Beat in the butter and egg yolks and finally the cheese. Taste for seasoning and add more salt if necessary. Cover and leave the mixture to cool to room temperature by which time it will have firmed a bit and be easier to handle.

Form the potato mixture into 14-16 croquettes, weighing about 50g each. Spread the flour and breadcrumbs on to 2 separate plates or shallow bowls. Beat the egg in another bowl.

Dip a croquette in the flour, pat off any excess, then coat it in egg. Finally, dip it in the breadcrumbs and place on a baking tray. Coat the rest of the croquettes in the same way, then put them in the fridge to firm up.

To cook them you have several options. One: preheat the oven to 200°C/ Fan 180°C/Gas 6. Put the croquettes on a baking tray and drizzle them with oil, then bake them for about 20 minutes until golden brown. Two: shallow-fry the croquettes in a large frying pan, turning them regularly so they fry evenly. Three: heat some oil to about 180°C in a large saucepan or deep-fat fryer and fry the croquettes for 3-4 minutes. Drain them well on kitchen paper and serve piping hot.

MOROCCAN PASTILLA

Pastilla, or bastilla, is a Moroccan pie, which looks dead impressive but is surprisingly easy to make. It doesn't matter if it's not that neat – we like rustic. We used pistachio nuts when we cooked this in Fez for our telly show, but the locals prefer almonds. The choice is yours.

SERVES 4

1 tbsp olive oil

4–6 boneless chicken thighs (about 750g)

10g butter

2 onions, finely chopped

2 garlic cloves, finely chopped

1 tsp ground ginger

½ tsp cinnamon

½ tsp turmeric

pinch of saffron

500ml chicken stock

4 eggs, beaten

75g ground almonds or pistachios

75g dried dates, finely chopped

1 tbsp orange blossom water

1 tsp orange zest

4 tbsp finely chopped parsley

sea salt and freshly ground black pepper

TO ASSEMBLE

6 large slices of filo pastry

60g butter, melted

1 tbsp icing sugar

pinch of cinnamon

Heat the oil in a large frying pan. Add the chicken and fry it skin-side down, until crisped up and brown. Turn the thighs over and cook for a couple more minutes, then remove them from the pan. Add the butter to the pan and when it has melted, add the onions and fry them gently until soft. Add the garlic and spices and fry for a couple more minutes.

Put the chicken back in the pan and pour in the stock or 500ml of water. Season, then cover the pan and simmer for about half an hour or until the chicken is tender. Remove the chicken and set it aside. When it is cool enough to handle, finely chop the meat – it's up to you whether you keep the skin or not. Put the liquid back over the heat and reduce it by half.

Add the eggs to the cooking liquid and continue to cook over a low heat until you have a mixture that resembles loose scrambled eggs. Add the ground nuts and stir, then add the dates, orange blossom water, zest, parsley and the chicken. Remove the pan from the heat and allow to cool.

Preheat the oven to 180°C/Fan 160°C/Gas 4. To assemble the pie, you need a large ovenproof dish about 28cm in diameter.

Take a sheet of filo pastry and brush it with melted butter. Drape it over the dish, making sure it is gently pushed into the corners without any tearing. Repeat with another sheet of filo, this time placing it at a right angle to the first. Repeat with a further 2 sheets of filo, this time placing them on the diagonal.

Spread the filling over the pastry. Fold over the overhanging pieces of filo in reverse order – they should just about cover the filling. Take the remaining 2 pieces of filo and cut them to fit the dish. Brush them with butter, then cover the pie, tucking under any corners. Bake the pie in the oven for about 30 minutes until the pastry is a crisp, golden brown. Remove from the oven and allow to cool a little before dusting it with the icing sugar and cinnamon.

CHICKEN, SAGE *and* ONION PASTIES

We don't know what they're going to say about these in Cornwall, but we're dead chuffed with them. We've used the traditional pasty method, but the mixture of chicken and squash is lighter than the usual beef and swede and tastes really good. The sage adds a nice touch too.

————————————————— MAKES 6-8 —————————————————

200g butternut squash, diced

200g potatoes, diced (about 1 large)

1 onion, finely chopped

300g chicken meat (thighs, breasts or a mixture), finely diced

1 garlic clove, finely chopped

2 tsp dried sage

2 tbsp plain flour

sea salt and freshly ground black pepper

PASTRY

450g plain flour, plus extra for dusting

1 tsp baking powder

225g butter, chilled and diced

2 egg yolks

beaten egg, to glaze

First make the pastry. Put the flour and baking powder in a bowl and add a good pinch of salt. Rub in the butter until the mixture resembles fine breadcrumbs, then add the egg yolks. Mix in the yolks with a knife, then add a small amount of chilled water, a very little at a time, until the dough comes together. Wrap the dough in cling film and chill it for half an hour.

To make the filling, put the squash, potatoes, onion, chicken and garlic in a bowl. Season with salt and pepper, then sprinkle in the sage and the flour. Toss everything together until well combined. Preheat the oven to 200°C/Fan 180°C/Gas 6.

Roll the pastry out on a floured surface. Cut out rounds of about 15cm in diameter – you should get at least 6 and probably 8 from this amount of pastry. Divide the mixture between the rounds, placing it in a line down the middle of each one and making sure you leave a good border at the ends. Brush the exposed pastry with the beaten egg, then bring the edges together around the filling. Press the edges together firmly and crimp them like a traditional Cornish pasty.

Brush the sealed pasties with beaten egg, place them on a baking tray and bake in the oven for about 45 minutes. To check the pasties are done, pierce one with a skewer, hold it there for 10 seconds, then remove it – the tip should be too hot to hold comfortably for more than a second. These are delicious hot or cold.

MEDITERRANEAN CHICKEN TART

A Mediterranean beauty – think Sophia Loren in a crust! We love the flavours in this and if you like, you could spread some pesto or sun-dried tomato paste over the pastry before adding the topping. Makes a great lunch with a little salad.

SERVES 4-6

large sheet of ready-rolled puff pastry

1 small red onion, very finely sliced

1 roasted red pepper, cut into thin strips

1 courgette, finely sliced into rounds

300g cooked chicken, sliced

2 tbsp olive oil

zest of 1 lemon

1 tbsp lemon juice

1 garlic clove, grated

1 tbsp thyme sprigs

1 tsp dried oregano, or fresh equivalent

4 medium tomatoes, sliced, or 100g cherry tomatoes, halved

a few black olives

a few basil leaves

beaten egg, to glaze

1 tbsp pine nuts

sea salt and freshly ground black pepper

Preheat the oven to 200°C/Fan 180°C/Gas 6.

Unroll the puff pastry on to a baking tray and score a 2cm border on all sides, making sure you don't cut all the way through. Lightly prick all over the base inside the borders with a fork.

Put the onion, red pepper, courgette and chicken in a bowl and season with salt and pepper. Whisk a tablespoon of the oil with the lemon zest and juice and the garlic, then pour this over the vegetables and chicken. Mix thoroughly until everything is well coated, then add the thyme and oregano.

Spread the vegetables and chicken over the puff pastry, staying within the border. Arrange the tomatoes and olives on top, then shred the basil and add this too.

Drizzle over the remaining oil and brush the border of the pastry with beaten egg. Bake the tart in the oven for 25-30 minutes, until the pastry is puffed up and golden brown and the vegetables are starting to char a little. Take the tart out, sprinkle the pine nuts over the top and put it back in the oven for a further 5 minutes.

CASSEROLES
and BRAISES

POSH CHICKEN FRICASSÉE *with* ARTICHOKES

This really does do a chicken breast justice. We cooked it in France with poulet de Bresse, one of the fanciest of all chickens, but just use the best you can find. Lovely with new potatoes roasted with olive oil and rosemary. If it's not artichoke season, you can substitute frozen artichoke bottoms or use those little artichokes in jars.

SERVES 4

4 boneless chicken breasts, skin on or off

4 globe artichokes

2 lemons

25g flour

50g butter

2 tbsp olive oil

1 shallot, finely diced

2 garlic cloves, crushed

200g mushrooms, wiped and sliced

200ml dry white wine

zest of 1 lemon

torn basil leaves or chopped parsley or both

sea salt and freshly ground black pepper

If you have time, brine the chicken to keep it plump and moist (see page 364). Meanwhile, tackle your artichokes. This is our special method.

Cut off the stalk about 1cm from the globe. Peel off the outer leaves, rubbing on lemon juice as you go to stop the artichoke going black. When you reach the heart, cut off the top about a third of the way up from the base and discard the top two-thirds. Take a melon baller or a spoon and dig out the choke – the fuzzy hairy centre. With a small knife, carve off the outer skin of the heart, then rub it with lemon juice. Prepare the rest of the artichokes in the same way and cut each one into about 6 slices. Bring a shallow pan of water to a simmer and add a good squeeze of lemon juice. Add the artichoke slices and simmer them for about 5 minutes, then cover the pan and set aside.

Blot the chicken breasts dry on kitchen paper, place them between a couple of pieces of cling film and beat them out briefly. Spread the flour out on a plate, season it, then coat the chicken in the flour.

Heat half the butter and a tablespoon of oil in a heavy-bottomed frying pan with a lid. Add the chicken and cook for a minute or so until golden, then turn it over, put the lid on the pan and cook gently for 10 minutes. Remove the chicken, wrap it all in foil and leave it to rest for 10 minutes.

Heat the rest of the butter and oil in the pan and gently cook the shallot for about 5 minutes until translucent. Add the garlic and cook for another minute, then add the artichokes and mushrooms and cook them until they start to colour. Pour in the wine and a tablespoon of lemon juice and cook until the liquid has reduced by half. Remove the pan from the heat and gently stir in the grated zest of one lemon and the herbs. Divide the artichokes and mushrooms between 4 plates, top with a chicken breast and drizzle over the resting juices.

CHICKEN *with* CHICKPEAS *and* APRICOTS

Pomegranate molasses is easy to find in supermarkets now and makes a great addition to this Moroccan-inspired chicken dish. The cayenne balances out the sweetness of the molasses and the apricots. We like chicken thighs for this, but you can use a mix of breast and thigh meat if you prefer.

SERVES 4

2 tbsp olive oil

2 red onions, sliced

2 garlic cloves, finely chopped

1 tsp ground ginger

1 tsp turmeric

1 tsp ground coriander

¼ tsp cayenne

¼ tsp cinnamon

¼ tsp cloves

500g boneless chicken thighs, diced

300ml chicken stock

100g dried apricots

400g can of chickpeas, drained

200g chopped tomatoes

1 tbsp pomegranate molasses

2 roasted red peppers, cut into strips

sea salt and freshly ground black pepper

COUSCOUS

200g couscous

1 tbsp olive oil

15g butter

handful of chopped parsley and mint

½ pomegranate

50g flaked almonds

Heat the olive oil in a large flameproof casserole dish. Add the onions and fry them gently for a few minutes until they're starting to soften. Add the garlic and spices and cook for a couple more minutes, then add the chicken to the dish. Stir for a minute to cover the chicken with the spices, then season with salt and pepper.

Pour in the chicken stock. Cut the apricots in half lengthways and add them to the pan with the chickpeas, tomatoes and pomegranate molasses. Bring everything to the boil, then turn the heat down and put a lid on the dish. Cook for about 20 minutes, then remove the lid and add the peppers. Cook for another 5 minutes, uncovered.

While the chicken is cooking, prepare the couscous. Put the couscous in a bowl with 200ml of hot water, then add the olive oil and butter and season with salt and pepper. Cover the bowl with cling film and leave the couscous to swell up for 5 minutes. Fluff the couscous with a fork, then stir in the chopped herbs. Remove the seeds from the pomegranate and toast the almonds in a dry pan, then scatter them over the couscous. Serve with the chicken.

CHICKEN PROVENÇAL

The best olives to use for this are the dry kind. You want the black ones, not in brine, which are an intense colour and are very slightly pitted or wrinkly looking. Polenta is the perfect accompaniment to this tasty dish.

SERVES 4

3 tbsp olive oil

1 onion, thinly sliced

1 red pepper, deseeded and sliced lengthways

2 garlic cloves, finely chopped

4 chicken legs or 8 thighs, skin on and bone in

a few sprigs of fresh oregano or marjoram

a few sprigs of fresh thyme or rosemary

zest of 1 lemon

200ml white wine

100ml chicken stock

4 small vines of cherry tomatoes

1 tsp balsamic vinegar

2 tbsp capers, rinsed

2 tbsp black olives, pitted and chopped

sea salt and freshly ground black pepper

POLENTA

200g polenta

50g butter

25g Parmesan cheese, grated (optional)

Heat a tablespoon of oil in a large frying pan that has a lid. Add the onion and red pepper and cook over a medium heat, stirring regularly, until both are starting to soften and brown. Add the garlic and fry for another minute. Tip the contents of the pan on to a plate and set aside.

Heat another tablespoon of oil in the pan. Season the chicken, then add it to the pan, skin-side down. Fry the chicken pieces for several minutes, until the skin is crisp and brown, then flip them over and cook them on the other side for a few minutes. Put the onion, pepper and garlic back in the pan. Add the herbs and zest, then pour over the white wine and the stock or 100ml of water. Partially cover the pan with the lid, and leave to cook for 25–30 minutes until the chicken is tender and cooked through.

Meanwhile, preheat the oven to 200°C/180°C Fan/Gas 6 and put the tomatoes in an ovenproof dish or tin. Drizzle the remaining oil and the vinegar over them and season with salt. Roast the tomatoes in the oven for about 8 minutes until they are on the verge of bursting, then remove them from the oven and set aside.

Add the capers and olives to the pan with the chicken and simmer, uncovered, for another couple of minutes. Serve the chicken with the tomatoes on the side and the polenta.

For the polenta, pour a litre of just-boiled water into a saucepan and bring it back to the boil. Add salt, then pour in the polenta and whisk until it has combined with the water and started to thicken. Turn the heat down and continue to cook for 20–40 minutes, whisking at regular intervals, until the polenta has a consistency similar to mashed potatoes and comes away from the sides of the pan. The exact timing will depend on whether you are using fine or coarse polenta. Whisk in the butter and Parmesan, if using, and transfer to a warm, lidded bowl. The polenta will firm up as it cools so is best served immediately.

COQ AU RIESLING

This is a twist on our beloved coq au vin. The great thing is because you use white wine instead of red you can add cream and the dish doesn't go a funny colour – and it tastes great. If you've time, we really recommend marinating the chicken but you can skip this if you're in a rush.

1 chicken, cut into 8 or 8 thighs or legs, skin on and bone in

bouquet garni made up of 3 bay leaves, 1 sprig of thyme and 1 sprig of parsley

750ml Riesling wine

1 tbsp olive oil

100g unsmoked bacon lardons

1 onion, finely chopped

15g butter

200g button mushrooms, wiped and left whole

3 garlic cloves, finely chopped

1 egg yolk

100ml single cream

handful of finely chopped parsley, to garnish

sea salt and freshly ground black pepper

Put the chicken pieces in a large bowl and season them with salt and pepper. Add the bouquet garni and pour over the wine, then leave the chicken to marinate for at least 12 hours if possible.

Heat the olive oil in a large flameproof casserole dish and add the bacon and onion. Cook over a medium heat until the onion has softened and browned slightly. Add the butter, then when it has melted, add the button mushrooms and brown them quickly over a medium heat. Remove the bacon, onions and mushrooms from the casserole dish with a slotted spoon and set them aside.

Remove the chicken pieces from the marinade and pat them dry with kitchen paper. Reserve the marinade. Put the chicken in the pan, skin-side down, and fry it until the skin is well browned. This will take at least 15 minutes on each side over a medium heat. When the chicken is a beautiful golden brown, add the garlic and cook it briefly for a minute or so, then put the bacon, onion and mushrooms back in the casserole dish.

Pour over the marinade and bring it to the boil. Turn the heat down to a simmer, cover the pan and cook gently for about 45 minutes, until the meat is almost falling off the bone. Carefully remove the chicken from the casserole and set it aside for a few minutes.

Whisk the egg yolk with the single cream, then pour this into the casserole dish. Cook very gently for a few minutes, until the sauce has thickened a little, then put the chicken back in the dish.

Serve sprinkled with parsley with buttered noodles or some mashed potatoes on the side.

CHICKEN *with* PEAS *and* BACON

Nothing exotic in this recipe – just chicken, herbs and veg – but the whole thing comes together to make a really fab one-pot supper that everyone will enjoy. Some mash alongside would be good.

SERVES 4

1 tbsp olive oil

150g unsmoked bacon lardons

8 chicken thighs, bone in and skin on

15g butter

2 leeks, cut into rounds

a few slender baby carrots, green tops attached, if possible

2 garlic cloves, finely chopped

1 sprig of tarragon

1 sprig of thyme

100ml white wine

250ml chicken stock

200g frozen peas

75ml crème fraiche

finely chopped parsley, to serve (optional)

sea salt and freshly ground black pepper

Heat the olive oil in a large casserole dish or a frying pan with a lid. Add the bacon and fry it until crisp. Remove the bacon from the pan with a slotted spoon and set it aside.

Add the chicken thighs to the pan, skin-side down. Fry them over a medium heat for at least 10 minutes until the skin is crisp and brown, then turn them over and fry for a couple of minutes on the other side. Remove the chicken from the pan and set it aside.

Spoon off any excess fat from the pan and discard it, then add the butter. When it has melted, add the leeks, carrots and garlic. Turn them to coat them in the butter, then add the tarragon and thyme. Turn up the heat, pour in the white wine and when it's bubbled up a bit, pour in the chicken stock and add the peas. Season with salt and pepper.

Return the chicken to the pan, skin-side up. Partially cover the pan, then leave to simmer gently for about 30 minutes, by which time the vegetables should be tender and the chicken cooked through. Put the bacon back in the pan and stir in the crème fraiche. Simmer for a few more minutes until the sauce has thickened slightly, garnish with parsley if you like and serve.

BRAISED CHICKEN *with* MUSHROOMS

We got this idea from one of the mums on our 'Mums Know Best' show and this is one posh bird! If you have some fresh morel mushrooms they are sensational, but any wild mushrooms are good. You can also use 30g dried mushrooms, soaked in 200ml just-boiled water for two hours, then drained.

SERVES 4

1 tbsp olive oil

10g butter

1 chicken, cut into 8 or 8 thighs or legs, skin on and bone in

2 shallots, finely chopped

400g wild mushrooms, sliced

200ml dry white wine or sherry

200ml chicken stock

bouquet garni made up of 1 bay leaf, 1 sprig of thyme and 2 sprigs of rosemary

100ml crème fraiche

2 egg yolks

a few chervil leaves or parsley leaves

sea salt and freshly ground black pepper

Heat the oil in a large flameproof casserole dish or a deep-sided frying pan. Add the butter, which should melt and foam up immediately. Season the chicken pieces with salt and pepper and place them, skin-side down, in the pan – they should fit in one layer so you might need to cook them in batches. Fry the chicken over a low heat for 10 minutes until the skin is crisp and brown, then turn and cook them on the other side for a couple more minutes. Remove the chicken from the pan and set it aside.

Add the shallots to the pan and cook them for several minutes until soft and translucent. Add the mushrooms and cook them for 5 minutes until golden all over. If using dried mushrooms, drain them and make sure they don't contain any grit. Add them to the pan and cook quickly for a minute until they start releasing juices.

Add the wine or sherry and boil fiercely until it is reduced by half, then add the stock and the bouquet garni. Put the chicken back in the pan and leave it to simmer for at least 30 minutes, until cooked through. When the meat is almost falling off the bones, remove the chicken from the pan and keep it warm.

Mix the crème fraiche with the egg yolks in a small bowl, then stir this into the pan juices. Simmer the sauce very gently, not letting it bubble, until it is reduced and thickened.

To serve, pour the sauce over the chicken and garnish with freshly torn chervil or parsley.

CHICKEN NORMANDY

'Chicken à la Normande' if you want to be proper French about it, includes all the ingredients traditional in this region of France – apples, cider, cream and brandy or Calvados. It's rich and warming and goes down a treat. Excellent with crispy roasted potatoes.

SERVES 4

1 tbsp olive oil

4 chicken legs or 8 thighs, skin on and bone in

4 banana shallots, sliced lengthways into wedges

large sprig of thyme

50ml brandy or Calvados

300ml cider

50ml crème fraiche

sea salt and freshly ground black pepper

APPLES

25g butter

2 eating apples, cored and cut into wedges

1 tbsp demerara or soft brown sugar

Heat the olive oil in a large flameproof casserole dish or a frying pan with a lid. Add the chicken legs or thighs and cook them for 10 minutes on each side, until they're well browned and the skin is crisp. Remove the chicken from the pan and set it aside.

If there is a lot of fat in the pan spoon some off – you only need about a tablespoon. Add the shallots and sauté them over a medium heat until very lightly browned. Add the thyme, then put the chicken back in the pan.

Heat the brandy or Calvados in a small saucepan or a ladle, then ignite it and pour the flaming alcohol over the chicken. Wait for the flames to die down, then pour in the cider. Season with salt and pepper.

Bring the liquid to the boil, then partially cover the pan and turn down the heat. Leave the chicken to simmer for about 30 minutes, then remove the lid and turn up the heat to reduce the liquid.

While the sauce is reducing, fry the apples. Heat the butter in a frying pan and when it's foaming, add the apples and sprinkle over the sugar. Fry the apples until they are very slightly caramelised and softened, but still keeping their shape.

Remove the chicken from the dish and keep it warm with the apples. Add the crème fraiche to the juices in the pan, then simmer gently until well reduced. Spoon the sauce over the chicken and serve. Good with some crusty bread to soak up the juices and a green salad.

CHICKEN PAPRIKA

We first cooked this years ago in Romania and after much tweaking we have come up with this new version that's really rich and wonderful. We find it's best to use both sweet and hot paprika. A word of warning – don't keep your paprika too long as it does go off.

SERVES 4

1 tbsp flour

8 chicken thighs, skin on and bone in

15g butter

1 tbsp olive oil

2 large onions, sliced into crescents

2 red peppers, deseeded and cut into strips

2 tbsp sweet smoked paprika

½ tsp hot smoked paprika (optional)

300ml chicken stock

75g soured cream or crème fraiche

a few dill or parsley leaves

sea salt and freshly ground black pepper

Season the flour with salt and pepper, then use it to dust the chicken thighs. Pat them to get rid of any excess flour. Heat the butter and olive oil in a pan wide enough to hold all the chicken in one layer and add the thighs skin side down. Fry them on both sides until crisp and brown.

Remove the chicken and set it aside, then add the onions and peppers. Sauté them gently over a low heat until soft and translucent, then add the sweet and the hot paprika, if using,. Stir them in and cook for another couple of minutes, then add the chicken stock. Season with salt and pepper, then lay the chicken pieces on top of the sauce, skin-side up. Simmer, uncovered, for about 30 minutes or until the chicken is cooked through and tender. If it looks like the sauce is reducing too much, partially cover the pan.

Remove the chicken from the pan and keep it warm, then stir the soured cream or crème fraiche into the sauce. Cook over a low heat for a couple of minutes, then put the chicken back in the pan. Sprinkle with dill or parsley and serve at once with some creamy mash, noodles or rice.

POULE AU POT

'Poule au pot' – or chicken in a pot – is a very traditional Sunday lunch dish in France. It's basically a simple stuffed, poached chicken with lots of delicious veggies – the ultimate in one pots. If you like, you could add the chicken liver to the stuffing.

SERVES 4-6

1 x 1.5–1.8kg chicken

250ml white wine

up to 1.5 litres chicken stock

bouquet garni made of 1 bay leaf, 2 sprigs of parsley, 1 sprig of tarragon, 1 sprig of thyme and 2 cloves

12 shallots or button onions, peeled and left whole

4 carrots, cut into chunks

3 celery sticks, cut into chunks

4 turnips, quartered

500g small new potatoes

sea salt and freshly ground black pepper

STUFFING

1 tbsp olive oil

75g bacon lardons

1 onion, finely chopped

2 garlic cloves, finely chopped

1 tsp dried thyme

2 tbsp finely chopped parsley

75g breadcrumbs

1 egg

First make the stuffing. Heat the oil in a frying pan and add the bacon and onion. Cook them gently over a low to medium heat until the bacon has crisped up and the onion has softened. Add the garlic and cook for a further minute, then stir in the herbs. Remove the pan from the heat and leave to cool. Put the breadcrumbs in a bowl and add the contents of the frying pan. Mix well, season with salt and pepper, then stir in the egg.

Put the stuffing into the chicken, then pull the loose fold of chicken skin over the entrance to the cavity and secure with cocktail sticks or skewers. This will help prevent the stuffing from getting soggy.

Put the chicken in a large flameproof casserole dish or a stock pot and season with salt and pepper. Add the wine and top up with chicken stock until at least two-thirds of the chicken is covered – add extra water if you need. Bring the liquid to the boil, then skim off any foam that appears on the surface. Add the bouquet garni and a teaspoon of salt, then partially cover the dish and leave to simmer for 45 minutes.

Add the shallots or button onions, carrots, celery sticks, turnips and potatoes, then simmer gently for another 30 minutes. Check if the chicken is cooked – the stuffing should be piping hot, any juices should run clear and the legs should feel loose. Once the chicken is done, turn off the heat and leave the chicken to stand for 15 minutes.

Remove the chicken from the dish, cover, and leave to rest. Remove the vegetables and keep them warm too. Put the dish of cooking liquor back on the heat and boil it fast to reduce and concentrate the flavour.

Serve the chicken with the stuffing and vegetables in shallow bowls with some of the cooking liquor poured over the top.

CHICKEN TAGINE
with preserved lemons and green olives

We love Moroccan food – it's full of sunshine and great flavours. Preserved lemons are a classic ingredient and you can buy them in most supermarkets now or make your own. We cooked this when we were filming in Fez and we reckon it was better than the one the locals made!

SERVES 4

2 tbsp olive oil

2 large white onions, finely sliced

3 garlic cloves, finely chopped

1 tsp ground ginger

½ tsp ground white pepper

¼ tsp cinnamon

¼ tsp ground cloves

1 chicken, cut into 8 or 8 thighs or legs, skin on and bone in

300ml chicken stock

generous pinch of saffron, soaked in a little water

2 preserved lemons, cut into strips

20 green olives, pitted

2 tbsp finely chopped parsley

2 tbsp finely chopped fresh coriander

sea salt

Heat the olive oil in a large tagine, a flameproof casserole dish or a deep frying pan. Add the onions and sauté them over a medium heat until softened and turning a light golden brown.

Add the garlic along with all the spices. Cook for a further minute, then remove everything from the pan and set aside. Add the chicken pieces, skin-side down, and fry them for a few minutes, then turn them over – you will probably need to do this in batches so you don't overcrowd the pan. Put all the chicken back in the pan with the onions and garlic. Season with salt, then pour the stock or 300ml of water into the pan and add the saffron and its soaking water.

Bring the stock to the boil, then turn down the heat and cover the pan. Simmer, turning the chicken over regularly, for about 45 minutes, until the meat is about to fall off the bone.

Add half the preserved lemon strips and the olives and simmer the tagine, uncovered, for 5 minutes. Stir in the parsley and coriander and garnish with the remaining preserved lemon strips, then serve immediately with some flatbread or couscous.

SEFFA

This is a very famous dish in Morocco and every family has its own recipe. It's basically chicken, or other meat, served with couscous and a sauce and garnished with almonds, sugar and cinnamon. Delicious! We cooked a proper authentic seffa with the wonderful Aicha Ehwidar, who we met when we were filming. In Morocco they cook this in a special couscousier so we've come up with a simpler version to cook at home in a sauté pan.

SERVES 4-6

olive oil

2 white onions,
finely chopped

1½ tsp salt

2 cinnamon sticks

½ tsp ground black
pepper

1 tsp ground ginger

½ tsp turmeric

1 generous pinch
of saffron

1 x 1.5kg chicken,
cut into 8 pieces

1 tbsp butter

sea salt and freshly
ground black pepper

COUSCOUS

400g fine couscous

1 tbsp olive oil

hot chicken stock

2 tbsp unsalted butter

TFAYA SAUCE

2 tbsp olive oil

4 white onions,
finely chopped

1 tsp salt

½ tsp ground cinnamon

1 cinnamon stick

small pinch of saffron

½ tsp ground ginger

First cook the chicken. Heat 2 tablespoons of olive oil in a large non-stick sauté pan and add the onions, salt, and spices. Cook gently for about 5 minutes until the onions are translucent. Remove the onions and set them aside, then season the chicken pieces with salt and pepper, add them to the pan and brown them on all sides for 10 minutes or until golden all over. You might need to do this in batches, adding more oil as needed.

Put the onions back in the pan with all the chicken and add enough water to cover the onions by about a centimetre (you'll probably need about 500ml). Add the butter, turn the heat up to medium-high, then put a lid on the pan and simmer for 30-35 minutes or until the chicken is cooked through. Check that the juices of the chicken run clear and no pinkness remains. If the chicken is not quite cooked, simmer for another 5 minutes.

To prepare the couscous, put it in a bowl, stir in the olive oil and season with salt and pepper. Pour over enough hot chicken stock to cover the couscous by a few millimetres, then cover the bowl with cling film. Leave the couscous to steam and absorb the stock for 4-5 minutes. Remove the cling film, fluff up the grains with a fork and stir in the butter.

For the tfaya sauce, heat 2 tablespoons of olive oil in large frying pan, add the onions and the rest of the ingredients except the sultanas and sugar. Cook the onions over a low heat for about 20 minutes, then add the sultanas, sugar and about 70ml of water and cook for another 10 minutes.

½ tsp turmeric

¼ tsp ground
black pepper

100g sultanas, soaked
in water for 30 minutes.

50g caster sugar

GARNISH

100g blanched
almonds, toasted
and ground

100g blanched
almonds, toasted

1½ tsp cinnamon

3 tbsp icing sugar

To serve the seffa, pile the couscous into a smooth mound on a large platter. Lay the chicken pieces on top and cover them with most of the tfaya sauce. Mix the ground almonds with half the sugar and cinnamon and sprinkle this on top of the sauce. Mix the blanched almonds with the rest of the sugar and cinnamon and arrange them in lines over the couscous. Serve any extra sauce in a bowl so people can help themselves.

BRUNSWICK STEW

Brunswick Stew is a traditional dish in the southern US and was probably first cooked in 1828 in Brunswick, Virginia for a hunting party. The meat used was most likely squirrel but now most people choose chicken! It was made for us by the Proclamation Stew Crew who regularly cook up huge amounts of this feast of a dish for special events in Virginia. We've adapted the recipe slightly to feed fewer people and to use ingredients available in the UK – hope you love it as much as we do.

SERVES 6-8

25g butter

3 rashers of streaky bacon, diced

2 small onions, sliced

1 garlic clove, crushed

1 tsp chilli flakes

6 skinless, boneless chicken thighs

1 bay leaf

500ml chicken stock

400g can of chopped tomatoes

1 tsp dark brown sugar

450g potatoes, diced

400g can of butterbeans, drained

326g can of sweetcorn, drained

2 tbsp chopped parsley

sea salt and freshly ground black pepper

Melt the butter in a casserole dish over a medium heat and fry the bacon until browned. Remove the bacon with a slotted spoon and set it aside, then add the onions to the dish. Gently fry the onions for a couple of minutes until they are beginning to soften, then add the crushed garlic and chilli flakes and cook for another minute or so.

Push the onions to the side of the dish and add the chicken thighs and the browned bacon. Season with salt and pepper, turn up the heat and add the bay leaf, chicken stock, tomatoes, brown sugar and potatoes, then stir. Bring the stew to the boil, turn down the heat, cover the pan and simmer for about an hour.

Add the drained butterbeans and sweetcorn to the stew, season again and simmer, uncovered, for another 20 minutes, stirring occasionally. By this time the stew should be rich and thick and the chicken tender and falling apart. Sprinkle with parsley before serving up in big bowlfuls.

MOROCCAN CHICKEN

This is a very popular Moroccan dish – the proper name is 'djej m'hammer'. The chicken is marinated, then cooked in two ways. First, it's cooked in a saucepan on the hob, then it's popped under the grill to brown. It was prepared for us in Morocco when we filmed there and it was oh so good. We've adapted the recipe slightly for you to cook at home.

—————————————— SERVES 4 ——————————————

1 x 1.5kg chicken

juice of ½ lemon

2 tbsp olive oil

2 onions, finely chopped

2 tsp ground ginger

¼ tsp ground black pepper

¼ tsp turmeric

½ tsp salt

pinch of saffron

2 garlic cloves, crushed

small bunch of parsley, tied with string, plus 1 tbsp chopped parsley

handful of green olives

MARINADE

2 tsp ground ginger

¼ tsp ground black pepper

¼ tsp turmeric

½ tsp salt

pinch of saffron

½ preserved lemon, finely chopped

2 garlic cloves, crushed

1 tbsp olive oil

Rub the chicken all over with lemon juice. Mix the marinade ingredients together and spread them over the chicken. Put the chicken in a bowl or a large plastic bag and leave it to marinate for at least an hour, or overnight.

Heat the olive oil in a large flameproof casserole dish over a low heat, add the chopped onions and fry them gently until they are starting to soften. Add the ginger, black pepper, turmeric, salt, saffron and garlic and cook for another minute.

Remove the chicken from the marinade and pour any excess liquid on to the onions. Push the onions to one side and add the chicken to the casserole dish. Gently brown the chicken for 5 minutes on each side, cooking the breast side first – it won't take on much colour at this stage. Then turn up the heat, add the bunch of parsley and enough water to come a third of the way up the side of the bird. Bring the liquid to the boil, then turn the heat down, put a lid on the dish and simmer the chicken for about 1 hour.

Preheat your grill to high. Remove the chicken from the casserole dish and put it in a roasting tin, breast-side up, then pop the tin under the hot grill for 5 minutes to brown the skin. When the chicken is brown, remove it from the grill and leave it to rest on a warm plate.

Meanwhile, take the bunch of parsley out of the cooking liquid and discard it. Put the casserole dish back on the hob, add the olives and turn up the heat. Cook until the liquid is reduced by half and you have a thickish sauce. This should take about 15 minutes.

When the sauce is ready, pour it over the chicken, garnish with the chopped parsley and serve.

GEORGES BLANC'S POULARDE *de* BRESSE

When filming in France, we were hugely honoured to visit Georges Blanc at his restaurant in Vonnas. Georges holds three Michelin stars and is one of the most respected French chefs. He cooked us this chicken dish with the famous Bresse chicken and he gave us his recipe so you can try it for yourself – we've adapted the recipe slightly for the home cook and to serve four. Vin Jaune is a very special wine made in eastern France, but it's fine to use a dry fino sherry instead.

SERVES 4

50g unsalted butter

1.8kg chicken, jointed into 8 pieces (2 thighs, 2 drumsticks and 2 breasts, cut in half)

1 onion, cut into wedges

2 garlic cloves, finely chopped

10 button mushrooms, wiped and cut in half

200ml Vin Jaune (or dry fino sherry)

300ml double cream

1 tbsp crème fraiche

200g asparagus tips

squeeze of lemon juice

1 tsp medium curry powder

2 tbsp freshly chopped tarragon

sea salt and freshly ground black pepper

MUSHROOMS

15g unsalted butter

1 round shallot, finely chopped

100g fresh morels, cleaned (or other wild mushrooms, sliced)

Melt the butter in a large non-stick sauté pan over a high heat. Season the chicken pieces and add them to the pan with the onion, garlic and mushrooms. Cook until the chicken is golden brown on each side and well coated in buttery juices.

Pour in the wine or sherry and let it reduce for a few minutes, scraping the pan to loosen the caramelised juices. Add the cream and the crème fraiche, then turn the heat down low. Cover the pan with a lid and simmer gently for 30–35 minutes, until the chicken is cooked through.

Meanwhile, bring a pan of salted water to the boil and blanch the asparagus tips for 2 minutes. Drain them and refresh in a bowl of iced water to stop them cooking any more. Set them aside

When the chicken pieces are cooked, remove them from the pan, transfer them to a plate and cover with foil while you finish the sauce. Pass the sauce through a fine sieve into a clean pan. Add the lemon juice and curry powder and check the seasoning, adding more salt and pepper if needed. Gently bring the sauce to the boil, then take the pan off the heat and set it aside.

Prepare the mushrooms. Melt the butter in a non-stick frying pan and sauté the chopped shallot until softened. Add the mushrooms and continue to sauté for a further couple of minutes. Add the mushroom mixture to the cream sauce just before serving, then add the asparagus tips, stirring to coat them in sauce, and the chopped tarragon. Warm the sauce through briefly if necessary.

Divide the cooked chicken between serving plates and spoon the sauce over the chicken and alongside.

FRIED, GRILLED
and BARBECUED

BARBECUED CHICKEN *with aioli*

Everyone loves barbecued chicken, especially with a big bowl of garlicky aioli to dip it into. But – and it's a big but – you do need to cook your chicken carefully so you don't end up with a burnt offering on the outside and undercooked pink meat on the inside. Follow our guidelines and you should be fine.

SERVES 4

1 chicken, cut into
8 pieces

75ml olive oil

juice of 2 lemons

1 tbsp dried herbs such
as oregano, rosemary,
thyme or sage

sea salt and freshly
ground black pepper

AIOLI

3–4 garlic cloves,
crushed

2 egg yolks

½ tsp Dijon mustard

pinch of saffron,
ground and soaked
with 1 tbsp warm
water (optional)

250ml sunflower oil

50ml olive oil

squeeze of lemon juice
(optional)

If you don't want to use a whole chicken, you could use a spatchcocked chicken (see page 370) instead or 8 chicken pieces on the bone. If you prefer your meat off the bone, you could use 8 boneless chicken thigh fillets (skin on) or 4 butterflied chicken breasts (see page 368) – skin on.

Whatever you chooose, put your chicken pieces in a large bowl and season them with plenty of salt and black pepper. Whisk the olive oil with the lemon juice and herbs and pour this over the chicken. Massage the mixture into the chicken and leave to it all to marinate for as long as you can – at least 2-3 hours or preferably overnight, unless you're using butterflied chicken breasts. They only need to marinate for an hour.

When you're ready to barbecue the chicken, drain it well – the oil could cause a flare up if you're not careful. Chicken on the bone is best cooked on an indirect heat to start with and covered with the barbecue hood for the first 20 minutes. Depending on how hot your barbecue is, the chicken should take 30-45 minutes with regular turning. Transfer the chicken to direct heat (directly over the coals) for the last 10 minutes to crisp up and blacken the skin. Check the chicken is cooked through, then remove it from the heat.

If you are barbecuing boneless chicken, the process is much quicker. Cook butterflied breasts and thigh fillets over direct heat, turning them regularly for 8-10 minutes for breast or 10-15 for thigh meat.

To make the aioli, put the garlic in a bowl with the egg yolks, Dijon mustard and the saffron and its water, if using. Add a generous pinch of salt and whisk until well combined. Start adding the oils, literally a drop at a time to start with, until the mixture starts to emulsify, then you can start adding the oil at a slightly faster rate. Continue until all the oil is added. Taste for seasoning and add a few drops of lemon juice if you like, then serve with the chicken.

CHICKEN SHWARMA *with Israeli couscous*

This is a hugely popular dish in Israel, where everyone argues about the best recipe. We're doing ours the traditional way – marinating whole boneless thighs, then slicing them – but if you like, you could dice the chicken before marinating, then thread it on to skewers. Excellent with labneh, a kind of strained yoghurt, and herby pearl couscous.

SERVES 4

8–12 skinless, boneless chicken thighs

pinch of salt

juice of 2 lemons

50ml olive oil

4 garlic cloves, crushed

1 tsp ground cumin

1 tsp ground coriander

1 tsp sweet smoked paprika

½ tsp cinnamon

½ tsp cayenne or red chilli powder

2 bay leaves, crushed

LABNEH

500g thick Greek yoghurt

½ tsp sea salt

The labneh (and preferably the chicken) needs to be started a day ahead of cooking. To make the labneh, line a colander or sieve with a double layer of cheesecloth or muslin and place it over a bowl – don't forget you need to be able to put the whole thing in your fridge. Pour in the yoghurt and add the salt. Wrap the cloth around the yoghurt and tie it into a bundle, then put it in the fridge to strain, preferably overnight, until much thicker but still creamy.

Put the chicken thighs in a large bag or bowl and sprinkle them with a good pinch of salt. Whisk the lemon juice and oil together in a small bowl, then add the garlic, all the spices and the bay leaves. Stir thoroughly, then pour the mixture over the chicken, rubbing it in with your hands. If you've put the chicken in a bag, you can seal it, then massage in the marinade from the outside of the bag if you don't want to get your hands greasy. Leave the chicken to marinate in the fridge for at least a few hours, preferably overnight.

Take the chicken out of the fridge and allow it to come up to room temperature before you start cooking.

If you are barbecuing the chicken, prepare your grill. Otherwise heat your grill or stove-top griddle to a medium setting. Scrape off any excess marinade from the chicken, then barbecue it on an indirect heat, or grill or griddle it, turning frequently, for 20–25 minutes. You don't want to cook the chicken too fast or it will toughen up and the outer layer will dry out before the middle is cooked through.

Remove the chicken from the barbecue or grill and leave it to rest for a few minutes, before slicing it and serving with labneh and the couscous.

ISRAELI COUSCOUS

2 tbsp olive oil

200g large pearl couscous

pinch of salt

½ red onion, finely chopped

zest and juice of 1 lemon

large bunch of parsley, finely chopped

small bunch of mint, finely chopped

small bunch of fresh coriander, finely chopped

sprinkling of sumac (optional)

Put a tablespoon of olive oil in a saucepan and add the couscous. Fry it for a couple of minutes until the couscous starts giving off a toasty smell, then cover it generously with water. Add salt, then bring to the boil and simmer for 6-8 minutes until the couscous is just tender.

Drain the couscous and transfer it to a bowl. Stir in the red onion, lemon zest and herbs. Whisk the remaining oil with the lemon juice and season. Pour this over the couscous and sprinkle with a little sumac if you like before serving.

PAN-FRIED CHICKEN BREASTS
with herbs and white wine

Sometimes all you want is something quick, simple but wonderfully tasty, and this is just the thing – fast food with class. The herbs are what make this dish, so it's well worth getting the full selection if you can. Serve with some fresh green vegetables and new potatoes or rice.

SERVES 4

4 skinless, boneless
chicken breasts

1 tbsp olive oil

150ml white wine

juice of ½ lemon

25g butter

small bunch of chervil,
finely chopped

small bunch of parsley,
finely chopped

a few sprigs of tarragon,
finely chopped

a few chives, snipped

sea salt and freshly
ground black pepper

Butterfly the chicken breasts (see page 368), then season them with salt and and pepper. Heat the olive oil in a large frying pan. Cook the chicken breasts for 3-4 minutes on each side until just cooked through, then remove, cover with foil and keep them warm. If your frying pan isn't large enough, you may have to cook the chicken in a couple of batches.

Add the white wine and lemon juice to the pan and bring to the boil, scraping up any sticky bits from bottom of the pan with a wooden spoon. Let the liquid bubble away until it is reduced by half, then add the butter. When the butter is foaming, add all the herbs and swirl to combine. Spoon the sauce over the chicken breasts to serve.

SOUTHERN FRIED CHICKEN
with sweetcorn fritters and waffles

This ain't great for the waistline but it sure is soul food. This is what we cooked on the American part of our chicken trip. We made our own little adjustments to the traditional recipe – marinating the chicken in buttermilk to make it extra juicy and adding a slug of Worcestershire sauce too. We find that part frying and part roasting the chicken gives good results and means you can cook more pieces at a time and so feed lots of greedy people!

SERVES 6

1.8kg chicken, cut into 8 pieces

250ml buttermilk

1 tbsp Worcestershire sauce (optional)

200g plain flour

2 tsp sea salt

1 tbsp paprika

½ tsp cayenne

1 tsp freshly ground black pepper

1 tsp dried thyme

1 tsp dried oregano (optional)

500ml sunflower or groundnut oil, for frying

Put the chicken in a bowl or shallow dish and pour over the buttermilk and Worcestershire sauce, if using. Toss the chicken in the buttermilk mixture, cover the dish with cling film and chill for at least 2 hours and up to 4 hours before cooking.

When you are ready to cook, put the plain flour in a large, shallow dish. Add the salt, paprika, cayenne, black pepper, thyme and oregano, if using. Mix them all together well.

Pour the oil into a large saucepan or a deep frying pan and place it over a medium high heat. Put a thermometer in the oil and heat to 180°C. Do not allow the oil to overheat and never leave hot oil unattended. Alternatively, heat the oil in a deep fryer.

Take a piece of chicken and shake it lightly to remove any excess buttermilk. Drop the chicken into the spiced flour and turn until it is nicely coated, then put it on a plate. Repeat with 3 more pieces of the chicken.

When the oil has reached the right temperature, carefully add the chicken pieces and cook them for 2–3 minutes on each side until golden brown and crisp. Remove the chicken and drain it on kitchen paper. Scoop out any bits of batter from the oil with a slotted spoon, then cook the rest of the chicken, making sure you bring the oil up to the right temperature in between batches. If it drops below 160° the chicken won't be as crisp.

Preheat the oven to 190°C/Fan 170°C/Gas 5. Put all the chicken on a rack and place it on a baking tray – this helps it stay crisp. Bake the chicken in the oven for 15 minutes or until cooked through.

Drain the chicken well on more kitchen paper and serve hot. Great with fritters, waffles and maple syrup.

SWEETCORN FRITTERS

MAKES 10

300g sweetcorn kernels
(frozen are fine)

3 spring onions, very
finely chopped

3 eggs

30ml milk

75g plain flour

½ tsp cayenne

vegetable oil, for frying

sea salt and freshly
ground black pepper

Put the sweetcorn and spring onions in a bowl. Beat the eggs with the milk, then pour this mixture over the corn and onions and mix well. Season with salt and pepper. Sift the flour and cayenne and stir it into the bowl.

Add oil to a large frying pan – you want to shallow fry these fritters, so make sure the base of the pan is well covered. Heat the oil, then test it by adding a tiny drop of the batter – it should immediately start bubbling around the edges when it hits the oil.

Using a small ladle, drop batter on to the oil – you need about 2 tablespoons of mixture per fritter so you can probably make about 4 at a time. Fry the fritters for a couple of minutes on one side until golden brown then turn them over and cook for a further minute. Drain the fritters on kitchen paper to blot off any excess oil and keep them warm. Continue until you have used up all the batter, then serve with the fried chicken.

WAFFLES

MAKES 8

50g butter

sunflower oil,
for greasing

150g plain flour

3 level tbsp cornflour

1½ tsp baking powder

1 heaped tbsp golden
caster sugar

pinch of fine salt

1 egg

225ml milk

maple syrup, to serve

butter, to serve
(optional)

Put the 50g of butter in a small saucepan and melt it over a low heat, then set it aside. Preheat the waffle maker to almost its highest setting and grease it with a little oil according to the manufacturer's instructions.

Mix the flour, cornflour, baking powder, sugar and a good pinch of fine salt in a bowl and make a well in the centre. Whisk the egg with the milk and melted butter in a jug until smooth. Then gradually whisk the mixture into the flour until just combined. Pour the batter into a jug and leave it to stand for 10 minutes.

Pour just enough of the batter into the waffle maker to fill each plate and quickly smooth the surface with a round-bladed knife or spatula. Close the lid and cook the waffles for 4-5 minutes or until well risen, crisp and golden brown. Lift the waffles out carefully with some tongs and keep them warm in a low oven while you cook the rest.

ISRAELI CHICKEN SCHNITZELS
with red cabbage and apple coleslaw

Schnitzels originated in Austria, where they were made with veal or pork, but now the chicken version is one of the most popular dishes in Israel. Coleslaw is the traditional accompaniment.

SERVES 4

4 skinless, boneless chicken breasts

50g flour

1 tsp smoked paprika

1 tsp mustard powder

½ tsp salt

100g matzo meal or fine breadcrumbs

1 tbsp sesame seeds

2 eggs

vegetable oil, for frying

RED CABBAGE AND APPLE COLESLAW

1 medium red cabbage (about 300g), shredded

1 carrot, cut into matchsticks

1 small onion, finely chopped

2 crisp eating apples, cored and finely chopped (not grated)

1 tbsp lemon juice

1 tsp caraway seeds

2 tsp cider vinegar

3 tbsp garlic mayonnaise (see page 354)

pinch of sugar

sea salt and freshly ground black pepper

Butterfly the chicken breasts (see page 368). Place them between sheets of cling film and flatten them with a rolling pin.

Spread the flour on a plate. Add the paprika and mustard powder, along with half a teaspoon of salt. Mix the matzo meal or breadcrumbs and the sesame seeds together on another plate. Beat the eggs in a bowl.

Coat each chicken breast with the flour mixture and pat off any excess. Dip them in the egg, then the breadcrumb mixture and set them aside.

Pour vegetable oil into a large frying pan to cover the base by about ½ cm and heat it to a medium temperature. This is important – if the oil is too hot the outside will burn before the chicken is cooked; too cool and the coating just absorbs the oil and you end up with soggy schnitzels.

Fry the chicken for 3-4 minutes on each side until it is a deep golden brown. You may have to do this in batches and if so, keep those you have already cooked warm in a low oven. Make sure the oil is the right temperature again before you cook a second batch. Serve hot with the coleslaw.

RED CABBAGE AND APPLE COLESLAW

To make the coleslaw, put the cabbage, carrot and onion in a bowl. Toss the apple in lemon juice, to stop it from browning, and add this to the cabbage. Sprinkle in the caraway seeds and mix thoroughly.

Whisk the vinegar with the mayonnaise, sugar and seasoning. Pour this over the cabbage mixture and stir thoroughly until it is all nicely coated.

BUFFALO WINGS

This American classic is a favourite of ours – and of everyone else too, we reckon. You can bake them in the oven if you like but we think deep fried is the business. And if you double fry them they are beyond good. Your butcher will split the wings into 'drumettes' and 'flats' for you.

SERVES 4

1kg chicken wings, tips removed and split into 'drumettes' and 'flats'

sea salt

vegetable oil, for frying

celery sticks

HOT SAUCE

50g butter

2 garlic cloves, crushed or grated

120ml hot sauce (an American brand such as Frank's is traditional)

1 tbsp cider vinegar

1 tsp sugar

sea salt and freshly ground black pepper

BLUE CHEESE SAUCE

100g blue cheese (a creamy one such as Saint Agur is good)

1 small onion, very finely chopped

100ml buttermilk

150ml crème fraiche

1 tsp cider vinegar

If you have time, prepare the wings by sprinkling them generously with salt, then lay them out on a rack in the fridge overnight. This will help them crisp up well when you fry them. An hour before you want to cook the wings, remove them from the fridge and allow them to come up to room temperature. Pat them dry.

To make the hot sauce, melt the butter in a small pan and add the garlic. Cook it gently for a minute or so, then whisk in the other ingredients. Taste for seasoning and add salt and pepper as necessary.

To make the blue cheese sauce, mash the cheese with the onion, buttermilk, crème fraiche and cider vinegar.

Half fill a deep fryer or a large saucepan with oil and heat to 160°C. Cook the wings in batches for about 10 minutes each batch, then drain them thoroughly on kitchen paper.

Raise the temperature of the oil to 190°C. Return the wings to the pan, again in batches, and cook them for a further 2 minutes until very crisp and a deep golden brown. Put the wings on kitchen paper to drain, then pile them into a bowl and smother them in the hot sauce. Serve them with the blue cheese sauce and some celery sticks on the side.

If you do want to bake the buffalo wings instead of frying, preheat the oven to 200°C/Fan 180°C/Gas 6 and cook them for about 45 minutes, turning them regularly.

SPICY KOREAN FRIED CHICKEN

This alternative KFC is set to take over the world – it's a dish that it's hard to eat in moderation. We first had this at the back of garage in Seoul and we have been converts ever since. Serve it up with the sauces and be prepared to get very sticky fingers.

SERVES 4

8–10 skinless, boneless chicken thighs

vegetable oil, for deep-frying

sesame seeds, for sprinkling (optional)

BRINE (OPTIONAL)

100g caster sugar

75g sea salt

FIRST COATING

35g plain flour

15g cornflour

½ tsp baking powder

½ tsp salt

BATTER

125g plain flour

25g cornflour

½ tsp baking powder

100ml vodka

If you have time, start by brining the chicken. Dissolve the sugar and salt in 200ml of hot water, then add another litre of cold water. Submerge the chicken and leave it for 2 hours.

To cook the chicken, drain and rinse it thoroughly if you've brined it, then pat it dry. To make the first coating, whisk the flour, cornflour, baking powder and salt together – this coating helps the batter to stick, otherwise it tends to fall off. Dust the chicken in this mixture, patting off any excess, and leave it to stand while you make the batter.

To make the batter, whisk together the dry ingredients, then add 100ml of ice-cold water and the vodka – the texture should be quite thin, rather like unwhisked double cream.

Half fill a deep fryer or a large saucepan with oil and heat the oil to 160°C. If you don't have a thermometer and you're using a saucepan, test the oil with a piece of bread – it should take around 30 seconds to turn a crisp golden brown; any quicker and the oil is too hot.

Dip the chicken pieces in the batter one at a time. Allow any excess to drip off over the bowl containing the batter, then slowly lower each piece into the hot oil, letting go when it is almost completely submerged. Fry for 8–10 minutes, then remove and drain on kitchen paper. The chicken should be cooked through but barely taken on any colour.

Now heat the oil to 190°C, or if using a saucepan, turn the heat up and leave it for about 5 minutes to reach the right temperature. When the oil is ready, fry the chicken for another 2 minutes until it has darkened. Remove and drain thoroughly. It should be beautifully crisp. Serve the chicken as it is with the sauces, or brush some of the sweet soy sauce over it and serve with rest and the chilli sauce. Sprinkle with sesame seeds if you like.

SWEET SOY SAUCE

100ml soy sauce

25ml mirin

25ml rice wine vinegar

20g root ginger, grated

2 garlic cloves, grated
or very finely chopped

50g brown sugar

pinch of salt

few drops of sesame oil

1 tsp cornflour

CHILLI SAUCE

2 tbsp Korean chilli
paste (Gochujang if
you can get it, or a
hot sauce or paste)

1 tbsp hot sauce

1 tsp rice wine vinegar

1 tbsp honey

a few drops of
sesame oil

sea salt (optional)

SWEET SOY SAUCE

For the sweet soy sauce, put the soy, mirin, rice wine vinegar, ginger, garlic and brown sugar in a saucepan. Stir over a low heat to dissolve the sugar, then simmer for a couple of minutes. Taste for seasoning, add a little salt if necessary and a few drops of sesame oil to taste. Whisk the cornflour with a little cold water until you have a smooth but very runny paste, then whisk this into the sauce over a low heat, until the sauce thickens very slightly. Set aside.

CHILLI SAUCE

For the chilli sauce, simply whisk all the ingredients together and thin with a little water if too thick. Taste and add salt if necessary.

CHICKEN KATSU DONBURI

This bowl of loveliness is a Japanese favourite and is basically delicious fried chicken that's cooked with a savoury sauce and eggs, then served over rice. It's actually very easy and the only thing to watch out for is that you don't overcook the eggs. Err on the side of softness as they will carry on cooking for a while once the pan is removed from the heat.

SERVES 4

2 skinless, boneless chicken breasts

2 tbsp flour

2 eggs

100g panko breadcrumbs

25g butter

100g basmati rice

1 tbsp vegetable oil

1 onion, finely sliced

4 eggs

sea salt and freshly ground black pepper

DONBURI (the broth)

1 tsp dashi granules

50ml light soy sauce

50ml mirin

1 tsp sugar

TO SERVE

shredded nori

Japanese pickles (such as ginger)

miso soup

First prepare the chicken. Cut the breasts as if you were butterflying them (see page 368), but instead cut them completely in half. Put each half in between 2 pieces of cling film and flatten them out with a rolling pin.

Put the flour, eggs and breadcrumbs on separate plates. Season the flour with salt and pepper, and beat the eggs to break them up. Dip each piece of chicken in the flour, then dust it off, dip it in the eggs, then finally coat with breadcrumbs.

Heat the butter in a frying pan. When it is foaming, add the coated chicken pieces and fry them for 2–3 minutes on each side until cooked through and golden brown. You might need to do this in batches. Place the cooked chicken on kitchen paper to drain, then set aside. Cook the rice in a separate pan according to the packet instructions and keep it warm.

For the donburi, put 250ml of water in a saucepan with the dashi, soy sauce, mirin and sugar. Bring it to the boil and simmer for 2–3 minutes.

Heat the oil in a large frying pan. Add the onion and cook it for a few minutes until softened. Cut the fried chicken into thick strips and arrange them over the top of the onion – try to keep the strips from each chicken breast close together and in the same formation to make it easier to serve at the end. Pour the simmering liquid into the frying pan and cook for another minute, then carefully pour the eggs into the pan around the onion and chicken. Cook until the eggs are starting to set, but are still quite runny – this shouldn't take more than around 30 seconds over a medium heat.

Make sure the rice is piping hot and divide it between 4 bowls. Top with a portion of the chicken, egg and onion mixture. Sprinkle with shredded nori and pickles, then serve at once with miso soup on the side if you like.

TANDOORI CHICKEN

We've done a few tandoori recipes in our time, but you can't have a book on chicken without this favourite so here's our latest version. Finger-lickingly good, we reckon. If you don't have Kashmiri chilli powder, use a mild red chilli powder.

SERVES 4

1kg chicken thighs or drumsticks or a mixture, bone in, but skinned

4 garlic cloves, crushed

30g root ginger, peeled and grated

150g yoghurt

2 tbsp lemon juice

a few drops of red food colouring (optional)

SPICE MIX

1 tbsp ground cumin

1 tbsp ground coriander

1 tbsp Kashmiri chilli powder

1 tsp ground cardamom

1 tsp turmeric

1 tsp sweet paprika

½ tsp ground ginger

½ tsp cinnamon

¼ tsp ground cloves

¼ tsp cayenne

sea salt and freshly ground black pepper

RAITA

200g natural yoghurt

2 tsp dried mint

pinch of sugar

First, make the spice mix by putting all the spices in a bowl with a teaspoon of salt and plenty of freshly ground black pepper.

Slash the flesh of the chicken pieces at intervals and put them in a bowl. In a separate bowl, mix the garlic and ginger with the yoghurt and lemon juice. Stir in the spice mix and the food colouring, if using.

Cover the chicken with the yoghurt mixture and mix well to make sure it is all covered. The best thing to do is to get in there with your hands and rub the marinade into the cuts in the flesh. Cover the bowl with cling film and leave the chicken in the fridge to marinate for at least 3 hours, but preferably overnight.

Take the chicken out of the fridge an hour before you want to cook it so it can come to room temperature. Prepare your barbecue. When the coals are hot, make sure they are either to one side or in the centre of the grill and place the chicken pieces so they are away from the direct heat. Cook, covered, for about half an hour, turning regularly and spraying with water on occasion until the meat is cooked through. Transfer the meat to the direct heat just to char it a little.

You can also bake the chicken in the oven or put it under the grill. To bake, preheat the oven to 180°C/Fan 160°C/Gas 4. Bake for 30 minutes, then turn up the heat to 220°C/Fan 200°/Gas 7 for a further 5 minutes.

To grill, preheat your grill to a high setting and cook the chicken for 10–12 minutes on each side. It should be cooked through and nicely charred in places.

To make the raita, mix the yoghurt with the mint, sugar and season with salt. Serve the chicken with lemon wedges and raita.

PIRI PIRI CHICKEN

This fiery Portuguese chicken dish has become a British passion – we can't seem to get enough of it. We like to make it at home with a spatchcocked chicken instead of pieces and we have fun tearing the lovely sticky flesh off the bones. Follow our instructions for spatchcocking on page 370 or ask your butcher to do it for you.

SERVES 4

1 chicken, spatchcocked

lemon wedges, to serve

watercress, to garnish

MARINADE

1 onion, finely chopped

4 garlic cloves, finely chopped

juice and zest of 2 lemons

generous dash of Worcestershire sauce

4 mild red chillies, deseeded and chopped

2 red bird's eye chillies, deseeded and chopped

2 tbsp white wine vinegar

1 tsp smoked paprika

1 tsp dried oregano

1 tsp soft light brown sugar

1 tsp salt

Put all the ingredients for the marinade in a food processor or blender and blitz until smooth. Put the chicken in a shallow dish and pour over the marinade. Massage the marinade into the chicken as thoroughly as you can, then cover it and leave it in the fridge to marinate for at least 3 hours, but preferably overnight.

Take the chicken out of the fridge an hour before you want to cook it so it can come to room temperature.

To barbecue, put the spatchcocked chicken on the grill and cook it for about 5 minutes on each side over the direct heat, then move it off to the side to finish off – it will probably take another 20 minutes of regular turning, but you can speed it up a little if you put the lid on your barbecue. Spray the bird regularly with some water or beer if it is browning too quickly.

To cook your chicken in the oven, preheat the oven to 200°C/Fan 180°C/Gas 6, then cook for 30–45 minutes.

Serve garnished with lemon wedges and sprigs of watercress.

SWEET AND SOUR CHICKEN

We all love getting this from the takeaway but you can make an even better version at home with nice fresh pineapple and not too much sugar. You can really taste all the different ingredients. If you thought you didn't like sweet and sour chicken, please try this one and you'll change your mind.

SERVES 4

½ small pineapple

2 skinless, boneless chicken breasts

2 tbsp olive oil

1 onion, cut into wedges

1 red pepper, deseeded and chopped

1 green pepper, deseeded and chopped

1 tbsp cornflour

4 spring onions, diagonally sliced (optional)

SWEET AND SOUR SAUCE

300ml fresh pineapple juice

1 tbsp cornflour

2 garlic cloves, crushed

25g root ginger, finely grated

1 tbsp dark soy sauce

2 tbsp white wine vinegar

2 tbsp soft light brown sugar

3 tbsp tomato ketchup

pinch of dried chilli flakes

freshly ground black pepper

First the sauce. Reserve 2 tablespoons of the pineapple juice in a small bowl. Add the tablespoon of cornflour and stir until smooth, then set aside.

Pour the rest of the juice into a separate bowl and stir in the garlic, ginger, soy, vinegar, sugar, ketchup and chilli flakes until thoroughly combined. Season with pepper and set aside.

Put the pineapple on a board and cut off the skin. Quarter it lengthways and remove the tough central core. Cut the pineapple into thick slices and set them aside. Cut each chicken breast into about 8 pieces. Heat the oil in a large frying pan or a wok and stir-fry the onion and peppers for about 3 minutes over a high heat. Coat the chicken pieces in cornflour and add them to the pan. Stir-fry for 4 minutes until very lightly coloured on all sides.

Add the slices of pineapple and the sweet and sour sauce to the pan with the chicken and bring to a simmer over a medium heat. Continue to cook for 4-5 minutes, stirring regularly until the chicken is cooked through and the pineapple is hot.

Stir in the cornflour and pineapple juice mixture and cook for 30-60 seconds until the sauce is thickened and glossy, turning the chicken and vegetables until nicely coated. Sprinkle with the spring onions, if using, and serve hot with some rice.

PAN-FRIED CHICKEN THIGHS
with bacon and red wine

Chicken thigh meat is just right for a dish like this, as it's juicy and has lots of flavour, more than a match for the bacon and red wine. Nice with some mash.

SERVES 4

8 chicken thighs, bone in and skin on

1 tbsp olive oil

1 small onion, finely chopped

150g smoked bacon lardons

2 garlic cloves, finely chopped

large sprig of thyme

200ml red wine

200ml chicken stock

25g butter (optional)

finely chopped parsley, to garnish

sea salt and freshly ground black pepper

Season the chicken thighs on both sides with salt and pepper. Heat the olive oil in a large lidded frying pan. Place the chicken thighs skin-side down in the pan and cook them over a medium heat until crisp and well browned – this will take at least 10 minutes. Brown them on the other side for another couple of minutes just to sear, then remove the chicken and set it aside.

Add the onion and bacon to the pan and sauté until the bacon is crisp and brown, then add the garlic and thyme and cook for a further minute. Pour in the red wine and chicken stock, and stir while you bring the liquid to the boil, scraping up any brown crispy bits from the base of the pan.

Sit the chicken on top of the contents of the frying pan. Turn down the heat, partially cover the pan with a lid and leave to simmer fairly gently for about half an hour. Check every so often to make sure the pan isn't too dry – add a splash of water or more stock if necessary.

Remove the chicken from the pan and whisk in the butter for a glossy finish if you like. Otherwise, just spoon over the pan juices and bacon over the chicken and garnish with chopped parsley.

CHICKEN ALMONDINE

We did this with fish last year but guess what – it works brilliantly with chicken too. The capers, herbs and lemon give it all a nice sharp twist. Good served with green beans and new potatoes.

SERVES 4

4 skinless, boneless chicken breasts

300ml buttermilk

50g plain flour

50g ground almonds

½ tsp dried rosemary, finely chopped

zest and juice of 1 lemon

1 tbsp olive oil

50g butter

30g flaked almonds

2 tbsp finely chopped parsley

2 tbsp roughly chopped capers

sea salt and freshly ground black pepper

Butterfly the chicken breasts (see page 368). Place them between 2 pieces of cling film and flatten them with a rolling pin.

Put the buttermilk in a shallow bowl. In another bowl, mix the flour and ground almonds with the rosemary and lemon zest. Season the mixture with salt and pepper.

Dip each chicken breast in the buttermilk and shake off any excess, then coat in the flour and ground almond mix.

Heat the olive oil and half the butter in a large frying pan. When the butter is foaming, add the chicken breasts, a couple at a time. Fry them for 3-4 minutes on each side until the chicken is cooked through and the coating is golden brown. Remove and keep warm while you cook the second batch.

Add the rest of the butter to the frying pan. When it has melted, add the flaked almonds and cook them for a couple of minutes until lightly browned. Add the parsley, capers and the lemon juice and warm through.

Serve the chicken breasts on warm plates, sprinkled with the flaked almonds, capers and pan juices.

DIJON GRILLED CHICKEN

This little dish is quick to do but has so much punchy flavour. You're going to love it. Nice with a tomato salad and perhaps some sautéed potatoes if you're feeling lavish.

4 tbsp olive oil

8 boneless chicken thighs, skin on

zest and juice of 1 lemon

1 tbsp red wine vinegar

1 tbsp wholegrain mustard

3 tbsp Dijon mustard

1 tsp dried herbes de Provence (or similar)

sea salt and freshly ground black pepper

Preheat your grill to a medium setting.

Heat a tablespoon of the oil in an ovenproof frying pan. Season the chicken with salt and pepper, then put it skin-side down in the pan and fry for 2–3 minutes.

Whisk the rest of the olive oil with the lemon zest and juice, the red wine vinegar, mustards and herbs. Add a little salt and some black pepper.

Pour this mixture over the chicken, then put the pan under the grill and grill the chicken for 10 minutes – or if you prefer, transfer the chicken to a baking tray, add the olive oil and mustard mixture, then put the tray under the grill. You will probably find the mixture separates a little but don't worry – it will be fine.

Turn the chicken over and baste it with the pan juices. Grill for another 5–6 minutes until the skin is a deep golden brown and the chicken is completely cooked through. Serve with the pan juices.

CHICKEN KIEV

This is our improved kiev recipe – our earlier one was good, but this one's a stonker. When you cut into one of these little beauties the garlicky filling oozes out and the aroma is unbelievable. This is a good dish for serving up to friends, as most of the prep can be done in advance.

4 skinless, boneless chicken breasts, with mini fillets

150g butter, at room temperature

50g hard cheese, such as Cheddar, grated

grated zest of 1 lemon

4 garlic cloves, finely chopped

a few rosemary needles, finely chopped

small bunch of parsley, very finely chopped

groundnut or rapeseed oil, for deep frying

50g flour

1 egg, beaten

100g fine breadcrumbs

lemon wedges, to serve

sea salt and freshly ground black pepper

First prepare the chicken breasts. Remove the mini fillet from the back of each breast and set them aside. Butterfly the breasts (see page 368), then put each one between 2 sheets of cling film and lightly flatten with a rolling pin. Don't make the chicken too thin as you may end up with holes that would allow the filling to leak. Do the same with the mini fillets. Sprinkle the chicken with salt and set aside while you make the filling.

Put the butter in a bowl with the cheese, lemon zest, garlic and herbs. Season generously with salt and pepper, then mix thoroughly until everything is well combined. Divide the mixture into 4 and shape it into long torpedos.

Take a butterflied chicken breast and put a torpedo in the middle of one half. Cover it with a mini fillet, then roll the chicken breast up tightly, tucking in any loose ends and making sure the filling is completely enclosed. Wrap tightly in cling film. Repeat with the remaining chicken and filling, then put them all in the freezer for half an hour to firm up.

Pour oil into a deep fryer or a large saucepan, making sure you don't fill it beyond the halfway point. Heat the oil to about 160°C – any hotter and the kievs will cook too quickly on the outside. Put the flour, egg and a quarter of the breadcrumbs on separate plates and season the flour with salt and pepper. Remove the cling film from the rolled breasts. Dip each one in the flour and pat off any excess, then coat thoroughly in egg, and lastly the breadcrumbs. Add fresh breadcrumbs for each breast so they don't get too messy.

When all the breasts are coated, lower them into the hot oil and fry for about 15 minutes. By this time the crust should be a deep golden brown, the chicken completely cooked through and the filling ready to run out as soon as you cut into the breast. Serve the kievs immediately, with some lemon wedges on the side.

NUTTY CHICKEN

Raj Chahal and Am Singh are two great cooks and they run a business called 'The Spice is Right', producing the best street food, such as chicken burgers, wraps and curries – all perfectly spiced, of course. We met them when we were filming an episode of our 'Chicken and Egg' TV series and they've let us share their very special recipe for a nutty chicken curry with you – it was passed down to them by Am's mother, Surinder Kaur. The fenugreek leaves really do make a difference to the flavour, but if you don't have any the dish will still taste good.

SERVES 4

3–4 tbsp olive oil

1½ tbsp ground cumin

2 tbsp tomato purée

8 green chillies, deseeded and finely chopped

2 tsp salt

2 tsp chilli powder

2 handfuls of fresh or dried fenugreek leaves (methi), washed, dried and chopped

2 tsp garam masala

20g root ginger, finely chopped

1.5kg skinless, boneless chicken thighs, diced

80g whole cashew nuts (dry roasted if you like)

Heat the oil in medium-sized wok or frying pan and add the cumin. Once it has browned slightly, add the tomato purée and green chillies, then mix everything well to make a paste. Add the salt and chilli powder and stir for 30 seconds, then add half the fenugreek, the garam masala and the ginger, while stirring.

Put the chicken in the pan and stir to coat it in the paste. Cook for 2 minutes over a high heat, then turn it down to medium and continue to cook the chicken. Keep stirring and moving the chicken around the pan. Do not cover.

After 12-15 minutes, check that the chicken is cooked through and add the cashews. Sprinkle over the rest of the fenugreek and the coriander, then serve with basmati rice and a bowl of yoghurt.

CHICKEN
with CARBS

CHICKEN PUTTANESCA *with* LINGUINE

We're big fans of puttanesca pasta sauce. It's really punchy and full of flavour and when topped with some chicken thighs it makes an epic dinner.

8 boneless chicken thighs, skin on

1 tbsp Italian seasoning (a mixture of basil, oregano and parsley)

4 tbsp olive oil, plus extra for drizzling

1 small onion, finely chopped

400g can of Italian cherry tomatoes

6 anchovy fillets, in oil

2 garlic cloves, crushed

½ tsp dried chilli flakes

250g linguine

1 tbsp baby capers

handful of fresh basil leaves, plus extra to garnish

sea salt and freshly ground black pepper

Preheat the oven to 180°C/Fan 160°C/Gas 4. Place the chicken thighs on a board, skin-side down, and sprinkle each one with a little Italian seasoning and some salt and freshly ground black pepper.

Carefully fold over the edges of each thigh into the centre, then tie tightly with kitchen string to make neat round parcels, with the skin on the outside.

Heat 2 tablespoons of the oil in a large frying pan. Add the chicken thighs, in batches if necessary, and cook them for 3-4 minutes on each side, or until browned all over. Transfer them to an ovenproof dish and set aside.

Heat the rest of the oil in the frying pan. Add the onion and fry for 3-4 minutes, or until softened.

Add the tomatoes, anchovy fillets, garlic and chilli flakes and continue to cook for 4-5 minutes, stirring well. Pour the mixture over the chicken, drizzle over a little more olive oil, then bake in the oven for about 20 minutes, or until the chicken has cooked through and the sauce has thickened up nicely.

Meanwhile, bring a large pan of salted water to the boil and cook the linguine according to the packet instructions. Drain well, tip it back into the pan and toss with a drizzle of olive oil.

When the chicken is cooked, remove the parcels from the sauce and take off the string. Stir the capers and basil into the sauce and season with salt and pepper.

Dish out the linguine, and add the sauce and thighs on top. Garnish with fresh basil leaves.

CHICKEN TAGLIATELLE *with* SAFFRON

This is a good one for people who aren't keen on tomato-based pasta sauces. The chicken juices and saffron blend beautifully to make a really tasty dish. It's simple to do, but there's no need to tell everyone that!

SERVES 4

2 chicken legs, bone in and skin on

1 tbsp olive oil

zest and juice of ½ lemon

sprig of rosemary

25g raisins

large pinch of saffron

250g tagliatelle

sea salt and freshly ground black pepper

Preheat the oven to 200°C/Fan 180°C/Gas 6. Put the chicken legs in a small roasting tin. Rub them with the olive oil, then season with salt and pepper. Sprinkle over the lemon zest and juice, then tuck the rosemary sprig underneath. Add 150ml of water to the roasting tin.

Roast the chicken legs in the oven for 30–35 minutes, until the juices run clear when a skewer is inserted into the flesh and the meat comes away from the bones easily.

Meanwhile, put the raisins in a small bowl with the saffron. Cover them with just-boiled water and leave them to infuse for half an hour. Cook the pasta in a large pan of boiling, salted water, according to the packet instructions – it should take 10–12 minutes.

When the chicken is cooked through, remove it from the oven, cover and leave it to stand for 10 minutes. Pull off all the meat, including the skin, and discard the bones. Set the meat aside.

Add the saffron, raisins and their soaking water to the roasting tin and set it over a low heat. Simmer, while stirring, so the juices combine, then check the seasoning. Drain the pasta and pour the pan juices over it, then stir in the chicken. Serve immediately.

CHICKEN RAVIOLI
with sage and mushroom sauce

There's quite a bit of work to making your own ravioli but it's deeply satisfying and you end up with a dead impressive dish. Put some music on, roll up your sleeves and enjoy. And if the ravioli come out as funny shapes, just call them rustic.

SERVES 4

PASTA

500g '00' pasta flour, plus extra for dusting

5 eggs

sea salt

FILLING

1 tbsp olive oil

10g butter

1 leek, finely chopped

100g chestnut mushrooms, wiped and finely chopped

1 garlic clove, finely chopped

1 sprig of fresh tarragon

400g chicken mince (half thighs, half breast, if possible)

100ml white wine

25g breadcrumbs

25g Parmesan, grated

25ml double cream

1 egg

sea salt and freshly ground black pepper

First make the pasta. Tip the flour into a mound on your work surface and make a deep well in the middle. Break in the eggs and season them with salt. With a fork or your fingers, break up the eggs and gradually start incorporating the flour into them. When most of the flour is mixed in, start working the dough into a ball. If the mixture seems a bit dry, flick a few drops of water over it. Knead until you have a smooth dough, then wrap it in cling film and leave it to rest in the fridge for an hour.

To make the filling, heat the olive oil and butter in a large frying pan. Add the leek and mushrooms and fry them gently until softened. Add the garlic clove and tarragon and cook for a further minute, then add the chicken mince. Cook over a medium heat, stirring regularly, until the mince has cooked through, then pour the wine into the pan. Season with salt and pepper and cook until the wine has evaporated. Remove the pan from the heat and leave the chicken to cool a little. Tip it all into a blender or food processor, add the remaining ingredients, then blitz to a paste. Transfer the mixture to a bowl and keep it in the fridge until you're ready to assemble the ravioli.

Cut the pasta dough into 4 equal pieces. Keep the pieces you aren't working with wrapped up so they don't dry out. Roll each piece out on a floured surface as thinly as possible – about 1mm thick is good. You can do this with a rolling pin or with a pasta machine if you have one.

Cut out rounds with a cookie cutter or even an upturned glass. We used a 7.5cm cutter and got 24 rounds from each piece of pasta. Put a heaped teaspoon of filling (10-12g) in the centre of half the rounds. Dampen the edges of each with a little water, then put another round on top and seal, making sure no air is trapped inside. Repeat until you have used all the pasta and filling. Crimp the edges with a fork.

SAGE AND MUSHROOM SAUCE

25g butter

1 shallot, finely chopped

100g chestnut mushrooms, wiped and finely sliced

1 garlic clove, finely sliced

100ml Marsala

250ml chicken stock

½ tsp dried sage

TO SERVE

1 tbsp olive oil

a few sage leaves

The ravioli can be cooked straight away, in plenty of boiling, salted water. It will only take a few minutes and when the pasta floats to the top, it is ready. Alternatively, you can keep the ravioli in the fridge for a couple of days or open freeze them before transferring them to a bag or container.

To make the sauce, heat the butter in a small frying pan. Sauté the shallot until soft, then add the mushrooms and continue to cook until they're softened. Add the garlic and cook for a further minute, then turn up the heat and add the Marsala. Let it bubble and reduce by half, then add the chicken stock. Season with salt and pepper, then add the sage and allow the sauce to reduce again by half. This will make quite a small amount, but it is very concentrated and buttery enough to coat the ravioli well.

For the sage leaves, heat olive oil in a small pan and drop the leaves in a few at a time. Remove them after 3-4 seconds and put them straight on to kitchen paper to drain. Garnish the ravioli with the fried sage leaves.

PASTA *with* CHICKEN LIVERS

Chicken livers are cheap and nutritious and just the job for anyone who likes a powerful, meaty pasta sauce. This is rich and decadent, but doesn't cost the earth, and it goes particularly well with the wide ribbony pasta called pappardelle.

SERVES 4

1 tbsp olive oil

10g butter

2 shallots, finely diced

50g pancetta, diced

1 garlic clove, finely chopped

300g chicken livers, trimmed and cut into bite-sized pieces

1 tbsp tomato purée

100ml vermouth or white wine

200ml chicken stock

a few sage leaves, finely chopped

squeeze of lemon juice

sea salt and freshly ground black pepper

TO SERVE

300g pappardelle or similar pasta

grated Parmesan cheese

Heat the olive oil and butter in a large frying pan. When the butter is foaming, add the shallots and cook them for several minutes, until softened, then add the pancetta. Turn up the heat a little to crisp the pancetta and give the shallots some colour. Add the garlic to the pan and cook for a further minute, then push everything to one side.

Add the chicken livers and cook them quickly on all sides to sear them. Season with salt and pepper. Stir in the tomato purée and keep stirring until it has coated the chicken livers well, then pour in the vermouth. Simmer until most of the vermouth has bubbled away, then add the chicken stock and sage leaves. Continue to simmer until the chicken stock has reduced and the sauce is slightly syrupy. Taste and adjust the seasoning, then add a squeeze of lemon juice.

Meanwhile, cook the pappardelle or other pasta according to the packet instructions. Serve the pasta with the sauce and plenty of Parmesan to sprinkle on top.

CHICKEN NOODLES

This takes no time to prepare and is very good to eat. One of the packs of mixed mushrooms you find in the supermarket works well or just use some shiitake and oyster mushrooms. Well worth getting your wok out for.

SERVES 4

200g udon noodles

½ tsp sesame oil

1 tbsp vegetable oil

2 skinless, boneless chicken breasts or 4 skinless, boneless thighs, cut into strips

400g mushrooms, wiped and trimmed, then sliced if large

bunch of spring onions, sliced, white and green parts separated

2 garlic cloves, finely chopped

10g root ginger, finely chopped

1 tbsp miso

150ml chicken stock

2 tbsp soy sauce

1 tbsp mirin

2 sheets of nori, torn into strips

sesame seeds

sea salt and freshly ground black pepper

Cook the noodles according to the packet instructions. They normally take about 10 minutes. Reserve 100ml of the cooking liquid, and toss the cooked noodles in the sesame oil.

Heat the vegetable oil in a large wok or frying pan. When the oil is hot enough (the air above it should start to shimmer), add the chicken and mushrooms and sauté them over a medium heat until the chicken is seared and the mushrooms have started to brown and soften. Add the white parts of the spring onions, then the garlic and ginger and fry everything for another minute.

Mix the miso with the stock and the reserved cooking water from the noodles and add this to the wok with the soy sauce and mirin. Simmer for a few minutes until the sauce has reduced a little and everything is cooked through. Taste for seasoning and add extra salt or soy sauce if necessary as well as plenty of black pepper.

Stir the noodles, nori and green parts of the spring onions into the chicken and mushrooms – the nori should wilt down immediately. Serve sprinkled with a few sesame seeds.

CHICKEN RISOTTO *with rocket leaves*

Risotto is one of the world's great dishes and so comforting – like a cuddle for your tum. It's easy to make but you just need a bit of patience as you stand there stirring the rice and thinking about life. You do need well-flavoured chicken stock – home-made is best (see pages 358–359).

— SERVES 4 —

1 tbsp olive oil

50g butter

1 large onion, finely chopped

2 garlic cloves, finely chopped

leaves from a sprig of thyme

grated zest of 1 lemon

300g risotto rice

1.2 litres chicken stock

100ml white wine

50g Parmesan cheese, finely grated

150g cooked chicken, torn or shredded into bite-sized pieces

100g rocket, roughly chopped

sea salt and freshly ground black pepper

Heat the olive oil in a large sauté pan or frying pan, then add half the butter. When the butter has melted, add the onion and cook it slowly over a gentle heat until soft and translucent. Stir in the garlic, thyme and a teaspoon of the lemon zest, then the rice. Continue to stir until the rice is glossy and coated with the oil and butter, then season with salt and pepper. Heat the stock in a separate saucepan and keep it simmering on the hob.

Turn up the heat and pour the wine into the pan with the rice. Let it bubble up for a minute until most of it has boiled off, then turn down the heat a little. Add a large ladleful of stock to the pan and stir continuously until it has all been absorbed by the rice, then repeat until you have incorporated all the stock. By this time the rice should be on the soft side of al dente with a very creamy texture.

Beat the remaining butter and the Parmesan into the rice quite vigorously, then fold in the chicken and about 50g of the rocket. Leave for a minute or so for the chicken to warm through and the rocket to wilt, then garnish with some lemon zest and extra rocket leaves. Serve immediately.

CHICKEN PILAU

Chicken, rice and herbs are a perfect combo and this is such a great supper – easy to cook and so satisfying. It is worth taking the time to remove the grey skins from the broad beans. They taste so much better that way and you get their lovely bright green colour.

SERVES 4

6 skinless, boneless chicken thighs, cut into bite-sized pieces

juice and zest of ½ lemon

100g yoghurt

1 tsp ground cardamom

½ tsp cinnamon

¼ tsp cayenne

pinch of cloves

1 tbsp olive oil

15g butter

1 onion, finely chopped

2 garlic cloves, finely chopped

400g basmati rice, very well rinsed

800ml chicken stock

100g baby broad beans, skinned

small bunch of dill

small bunch of fresh coriander

small bunch of parsley

sea salt and freshly ground black pepper

Put the chicken in a bowl and season it with salt and pepper. Sprinkle over the lemon juice. Mix the yoghurt with the lemon zest and spices, then pour it over the chicken. Mix everything together thoroughly, then cover and leave in the fridge to marinate for at least an hour.

Heat the oil and butter in a large flameproof casserole dish, add the onion, and sauté gently until soft and translucent. Turn up the heat, then add the chicken. Stir-fry briskly for a couple of minutes, then add the garlic and cook for a further minute.

Add the rice, then pour over the stock and season with salt and pepper. Bring to the boil, then reduce the heat to a simmer and cover. Leave to cook for 10 minutes, then add the broad beans. Cook for a further 5–10 minutes until all the liquid has been absorbed. Remove the pan from the heat and leave to stand, covered, for another 10 minutes so the rice can steam and dry out a little. It should be perfectly cooked.

Finely chop the herbs, reserve a spoonful, then stir the rest through the rice. Turn the pilau out on to a large serving platter and garnish with the reserved herbs.

CHICKEN BIRYANI

A biryani is really special and the ideal dish for a celebration. The leftovers are good the next day too – if there are any. We like to cut the chicken into quite small pieces for this – breasts into four, each thigh into two. Drumsticks can be left whole.

SERVES 4

1kg chicken pieces, bone in, but skinned

juice of ½ lemon

4 garlic cloves, crushed

30g root ginger, grated

1 tsp cardamom pods, seeds only

1 tsp fennel seeds

1 tsp cumin seeds

2cm cinnamon stick

½ tsp chilli powder or cayenne

½ tsp turmeric

200ml yoghurt

sea salt and freshly ground black pepper

RICE

500g basmati rice

2 mace blades

1 tsp green cardamom pods

3cm cinnamon stick

4 cloves

½ tsp black peppercorns

3 bay leaves

First marinate the chicken. Put the chicken in a bowl and season it with salt and pepper. Mix the lemon juice, garlic and ginger together in a bowl. Toast the whole spices lightly in a frying pan until aromatic, then remove them from the heat. When the spices are cool, grind them to a powder, then mix with the chilli powder or cayenne and the turmeric. Add this to the lemon juice mixture, then stir in the yoghurt. Rub everything into the chicken, then cover the bowl and leave the chicken to marinate for several hours, or overnight.

When you want to start cooking, wash the rice until the water runs clean and is no longer cloudy, then soak it in fresh cold water for 15 minutes. Put the mace, cardamom, cinnamon, cloves, peppercorns and bay leaves in a bag and pop it in a saucepan. Pour in plenty of just-boiled water and bring it back to the boil. Pour in the rice and season with salt. Simmer for 5 minutes only, then drain immediately and rinse under cold water.

To layer the biryani, heat 3 tablespoons of the oil in a large frying pan. Fry the onions over a low to medium heat until they have softened, then turn up the heat and fry quickly, stirring regularly, until they have browned and are slightly crisp. Put them on plenty of kitchen paper to drain, then mix half the onions with the rice. Set the rest aside. Add the green chillies and plenty of chopped coriander to the rice as well.

Grind the saffron with the salt and sugar, then put it in a small saucepan with the milk. Warm the milk through gently, then remove it from the heat and leave to infuse for half an hour.

Heat the remaining oil in a large flameproof casserole dish. Add the chicken and fry it on all sides until lightly browned. Add the stock and bring it to the boil. Simmer for 25 minutes until the chicken is almost cooked and most of the stock has been absorbed, then add the rice mixture, sprinkling it over evenly. Pour over the saffron and milk. Finally make holes with the handle of a wooden spoon and pour the melted butter into them.

FOR LAYERING THE BIRYANI

4 tbsp vegetable oil

2 onions, finely sliced

2–4 green chillies, finely sliced

small bunch of fresh coriander, chopped

pinch of saffron

pinch of salt

pinch of sugar

50ml milk

500ml chicken stock

25g butter, melted, or ghee

GARNISH

a few fresh coriander sprigs

a few mint sprigs

3 eggs, hard-boiled and cut into quarters

2 tbsp flaked almonds, lightly toasted

Place a folded tea towel or several sheets of kitchen paper over the casserole dish and place the lid on top. Place the dish over a low heat to steam for about 20 minutes, until the rice is completely cooked and the grains are separate. Remove from the heat and leave, covered, for another 10 minutes.

Spoon the biryani on to a large serving platter and garnish with the herbs, hard-boiled eggs, reserved fried onions and flaked almonds.

CHICKEN MAQLUBA

This is an amazing Palestinian recipe, made up of layers of chicken, vegetables and rice that are all cooked in a pot, then turned out like a layered cake. It is quite fiddly but truly spectacular and a great dish for a special occasion. It's best made in a wide, deep, lidded frying pan.

SERVES 4-6

butter, for greasing

1 large aubergine, sliced into rounds

4 tbsp olive oil

8 skinless, boneless chicken thighs

1 large onion, thickly sliced

2 bay leaves

½ tsp turmeric

½ tsp cinnamon

½ tsp ground cardamom

pinch of cloves

4 garlic cloves, sliced

up to 1 litre chicken stock

2 medium tomatoes, sliced

300g basmati rice, well rinsed

20g butter

pinch of saffron

25g pine nuts

a few sprigs of parsley and coriander, to garnish

sea salt and freshly ground black pepper

Butter your frying pan and line it with baking parchment. Butter the baking parchment too.

Preheat the oven to 200°C/Fan 180°C/Gas 6. Arrange the aubergine slices over a baking tray, brush them with olive oil and sprinkle them with salt. Roast them in the oven for about 30 minutes, turning them once or twice until the slices are well coloured, soft and still plump. Remove them from the oven and set them aside.

Heat the rest of the olive oil in a large casserole dish or saucepan. Add the chicken thighs and cook them on both sides for a few minutes until browned, then remove them and set aside. Add the onion and sauté for a few minutes until lightly golden, then stir in the bay leaves, spices and garlic. Stir for a minute or so, then put the chicken back in the casserole and pour in the stock. Cover and simmer for about 10 minutes. Remove the chicken and onion from the stock and set them aside.

To assemble the maqluba, arrange the aubergine and tomato slices over the base of the lined pan - it's fine to overlap them. Add the chicken, making sure some will be visible in any gaps between the tomatoes and aubergines when you turn the maqluba out. Sprinkle the onion on top.

Sprinkle over the rice, making sure it covers the vegetables and chicken in an even layer. Measure out 650ml of the chicken stock and pour it over the rice. Do this slowly and carefully so the rice doesn't float up and shift around. Press down on the rice with the back of a spoon so it is all completely covered and add a little more stock if necessary. Season with salt and pepper.

Bring to the boil, then turn the heat down to a simmer and cover the pan. Cook for 20-25 minutes, by which time the liquid should have been absorbed. Remove the pan from the heat and leave it to stand for a further 15 minutes.

YOGHURT SAUCE

small bunch of fresh
coriander, very finely
chopped

½ tsp dried mint

1 tsp ground coriander

1 garlic clove, crushed
or grated

1 tbsp lemon juice

300ml natural yoghurt

To serve, turn the maqluba out on to a large serving dish. It should drop on to it easily, thanks to the baking parchment. Peel off the baking parchment. Melt the butter in a small saucepan and add the saffron and pine nuts. Toast for a couple of minutes, then pour this over with maqluba and garnish with parsley and coriander.

To make the sauce, combine the ingredients and season with salt and pepper. Serve on the side.

HAINANESE CHICKEN

Chinese in origin, this dish is hugely popular in Singapore and in Malaysia. As the rice is cooked in the chicken broth not an atom of flavour is wasted. The sauce doesn't take long at all, but if you want, you could use ready-made sriracha sauce. Deseed the chillies if you can't stand the heat.

SERVES 4

30g root ginger

bunch of spring onions

1.2 litres chicken stock

3 garlic cloves, sliced

2 star anise

a few peppercorns

4 skinless, boneless chicken breasts

½ cucumber, peeled and sliced

fresh coriander, to serve

soy sauce, to serve

salt

RICE

15g butter

2 garlic cloves, crushed

10g root ginger, grated

300g jasmine rice

CHILLI SAUCE

2 very hot red Thai chillies, chopped

4 fat, milder red chillies, chopped

1 shallot, chopped

25g root ginger, chopped

4 garlic cloves, chopped

juice of 1 lime

1 tsp light brown sugar

Thinly slice the ginger, but don't bother to peel it. Slice the spring onions and set 2 of them aside to garnish the dish later.

Pour the stock into a saucepan and add the ginger, sliced spring onions, garlic, star anise, peppercorns and half a teaspoon of salt. Bring to the boil and simmer for 5 minutes, then add the chicken breasts. Immediately turn down the heat, cover the pan and simmer the chicken very gently for 7–8 minutes until just cooked through. Turn off the heat and leave the chicken to stand for 5 minutes. Remove the chicken from the pan and set it aside to cool a little. Strain the liquid into a jug and set it aside too.

For the rice, heat the butter in a lidded saucepan and add the garlic and ginger. Cook very gently for 3–4 minutes until the garlic has softened but hasn't taken on any colour. Add the rice and stir to combine until the grains are glossy.

Measure 550ml of the reserved stock and pour it over the rice. Season with salt, then bring the stock to the boil. Turn down the heat and cover the pan, then leave it to simmer for 10 minutes. Remove the pan from the heat and leave the rice to stand for another 10 minutes until all the liquid has been absorbed.

To make the chilli sauce, simply put all the ingredients in a small food processor with some salt and blitz until smooth. Add a little water or a tablespoon or 2 of the chicken stock if the sauce is too thick. Taste for seasoning and balance and adjust accordingly.

To serve, warm through the remaining chicken stock. Divide the rice between 4 bowls. Slice the chicken breasts on the diagonal and place the slices over the rice. Moisten with a little of the stock – you can also serve some in small cups on the side. Garnish with the reserved spring onions, slices of cucumber and fresh coriander and serve with the chilli sauce and soy on the side.

CHICKEN *and* SPELT RISOTTO

We're loving spelt - it's a very nutritious grain and makes an excellent risotto with great flavour and texture. What's more, you don't need to stand over this risotto, stirring it all the time - you just add all the stock at the same time and leave it to simmer. Easy peasy.

SERVES 4

1 tbsp olive oil

20g butter

1 onion, finely chopped

400g skinless, boneless chicken thighs, cut into thick strips

2 garlic cloves, finely chopped

200g chestnut mushrooms, wiped and sliced

½ tsp dried sage or a sprig of fresh

25g dried mushrooms, soaked in 100ml warm water

200g pearled spelt

100ml dry Marsala or sherry (such as oloroso)

800ml chicken stock

25g Parmesan or Pecorino cheese, grated

2–3 tbsp finely chopped parsley

sea salt and freshly ground black pepper

Heat the olive oil and half the butter in a large pan. When the butter has melted, add the onion and fry it gently until soft and translucent. Turn up the heat and add the chicken. Fry it briskly until seared on all sides, then add the garlic and chestnut mushrooms. Cook until the mushrooms have softened, then stir in the sage and season with salt and pepper.

Strain the dried mushrooms, reserving the soaking liquor but discarding any grit. Finely chop the dried mushrooms and add them to the pan together with the spelt. Stir until the spelt is glossy, then pour in the Marsala or sherry. Let the alcohol bubble off, then pour over the stock and the reserved mushroom liquor. Leave to simmer very gently until all the stock has been absorbed and the spelt is cooked. The grains should be swollen but still have a slight bite in the middle.

Take the pan off the heat and beat in the remaining butter and the cheese. Serve with plenty of parsley.

JAMBALAYA

This fantastic Creole dish comes from Louisiana and is a sort of paella, with attitude. There are all sorts of variations, but this chicken, chorizo and prawn recipe is our favourite. It's spicy, rich and gutsy – and it's a one pot!

SERVES 6

6 skinless, boneless chicken thighs

1 tbsp sweet smoked paprika

½ tsp cayenne

1 tsp garlic powder

1 tsp onion powder

1 tsp dried oregano

1 tsp dried thyme

1 tbsp olive oil

200g chorizo, skinned and sliced into rounds

2 onions, chopped

2 green peppers, deseeded and diced

2 celery sticks, sliced

3 garlic cloves, finely chopped

2 bay leaves

400g long-grain rice, well rinsed

400g can of tomatoes

1 litre chicken stock

12 large prawns, shelled and deveined

sea salt and freshly ground black pepper

TO SERVE

chopped parsley

lemon wedges

Tabasco sauce

Cut the chicken into bite-sized pieces, put them in a bowl and season with salt and pepper. Mix the spices, the garlic and onion powder and the dried herbs together and sprinkle half of this over the chicken. Rub it all in well and leave to stand for a few minutes. Set the rest of the spice and herb mix aside for later.

Heat a teaspoon of the oil in a large flameproof casserole dish. Add the chorizo and fry it quickly until it has browned on all sides and rendered plenty of fat. Remove the chorizo from the dish and set it aside. Add the chicken to the dish and fry, stirring regularly until seared on all sides. Remove the chicken and set it aside.

Check how much oil is left in the base of the dish and add the rest of the olive oil if necessary. Add the onions, green peppers and celery and sauté on a gentle heat for at least 10 minutes. The vegetables should be softening but without much colour beyond what they have picked up from the chorizo oil.

Add the garlic and the rest of the spice and herb mixture. Stir for a couple of minutes, then add the bay leaves. Return the chicken and chorizo to the dish, then pour in the rice. Stir for a minute, then add the tomatoes and stock. Season with salt and pepper.

Bring to the boil, then turn down the heat, cover the casserole dish and simmer for 20–25 minutes, until the rice has absorbed most of the liquid. Add the prawns and cook for a further minute, covered. Turn off the heat and leave everything to steam for a few minutes, by which time the rice will be fluffier. Stir the prawns through the rice.

Scatter with parsley and serve with lemon wedges and Tabasco for everyone to add at the table.

SPICY
CHICKEN

PEPPER CHICKEN CURRY

The marinade does the work for you here, adding flavour to the chicken and keeping it good and tender. Once that's done, the rest is a breeze. Great served with lemon rice.

4 skinless, boneless chicken breasts, cut into large dice

1 tbsp groundnut or sunflower oil

2–3 green chillies, slit lengthways, deseeded if you like

1 onion, finely sliced

1 green pepper, deseeded and cut into strips

1 tbsp yoghurt

1 medium tomato, finely chopped (optional)

juice of ½ lemon

sea salt

MARINADE

1 tbsp black peppercorns

½ tsp white peppercorns

1 tsp coriander seeds

½ tsp turmeric

25g root ginger, peeled and grated

6 garlic cloves, crushed

First make the marinade. Grind the peppercorns and coriander seeds until they're fairly fine, then mix them with the turmeric in a bowl. Stir in the grated ginger and the garlic and mix well.

Put the chicken in a bowl and season it with salt. Spoon over the marinade and mix thoroughly so the chicken pieces are well coated, then leave to marinate for a couple of hours.

Heat the oil in a large frying pan or a wok. Add the green chillies and cook them for a few minutes to flavour the oil, then remove them or leave them in – up to you. Add the onion and green pepper and fry them over a medium heat until they're starting to brown and soften.

Add the chicken to the pan and fry it quickly until brown on all sides. Stir in the yoghurt and cook until all the liquid has evaporated, then stir in the tomato, if using. Again, cook until most of the liquid is absorbed. By this time the chicken should be cooked through.

Sprinkle over the lemon juice before serving.

SHORSHE MURGI

Bengalis use a lot of mustard oil and strong flavours in their curries and this hot, fragrant dish is no exception. Yes, you do have to make a couple of pastes but you just blitz them in a food processor – there's nothing tricky.

SERVES 4

1kg chicken pieces, bone in, but skinned

1 tbsp mustard oil

½ tsp nigella seeds

2 black cardamom pods

3cm cinnamon stick

4 cloves

2 green chillies, slit lengthways

sliced green chillies, to serve

fresh coriander, to serve

MARINADE

1 tsp salt

juice of ½ lemon

½ tsp red chilli powder

½ tsp turmeric

1 tsp mustard oil

GINGER PASTE

1 large onion, chopped

4 garlic cloves, grated

30g root ginger, grated

MUSTARD PASTE

2 tbsp mustard seeds (yellow or brown or a mixture), soaked in water for half an hour

2 green chillies

First marinate the chicken. Put the chicken in a bowl and sprinkle over the marinade ingredients. Rub everything into the chicken, then set it aside while you make the pastes.

For the ginger paste, put the ingredients in a food processor and blitz with a splash of water until fairly smooth. Tip the paste into a bowl. For the mustard paste, drain the mustard seeds, then blitz them with the green chillies (deseed them if you don't want too much heat) with just enough water to make a paste. Tip that into a separate bowl.

Heat the mustard oil in a large frying pan. When it's hot, add all the whole spices and cook until the nigella seeds start to splutter. Add the garlic and ginger paste immediately and cook for a few minutes until the paste starts to separate. Add the chicken pieces and turn them until they are all coated with the paste and spices. Add the slit green chillies and cook, turning regularly, over a medium heat, for about 15 minutes.

Add the mustard paste and 300ml of water. Continue to simmer until the sauce has thickened to the right consistency – it should be thick enough to coat the chicken. Serve the curry with the sliced green chillies and plenty of fresh coriander.

CHICKEN VINDALOO

A curry house classic from Goa, vindaloo is one of our favourite curries – and once the marinating is done it's fairly quick to make. We know it's not traditional but we think some nutty brown rice goes well with this.

8–10 chicken thighs, bone in and skin on

2 tbsp vegetable oil or ghee

1 onion, sliced

2 green chillies, slit lengthways, deseeded if you like

20 curry leaves

400g tomatoes, peeled and chopped

MARINADE

1 onion, chopped

1 garlic bulb, cloves chopped

20g root ginger, chopped

100ml red wine vinegar

3cm cinnamon stick

1 tsp cumin seeds

1 tsp coriander seeds

1 tsp black peppercorns

1 tsp cardamom pods, seeds only

1 tsp fenugreek seeds

1 tsp mustard seeds

6 cloves

2 tbsp Kashmiri chilli powder

1 tsp turmeric

1 tsp sugar

1 tsp salt

First make the marinade. Blitz the onion, garlic and ginger in a blender with 2-3 tablespoons of the red wine vinegar to make a smooth paste. Toast all the whole spices in a dry frying pan until they smell aromatic. Be careful, as the mustard seeds will start to pop up at you. Grind the whole spices, then mix them with the chilli powder, turmeric, sugar and salt. Stir in the onion paste and the rest of the vinegar.

Put the chicken in a bowl, pour over the marinade and rub it in well. Cover the bowl and put the chicken in the fridge for as long as you can – preferably overnight.

Take the chicken out of the fridge an hour before you want to cook it so it can come up to room temperature. Put half the oil or ghee in a large frying pan. Scrape the marinade off the chicken and reserve it, then fry the pieces skin-side down until well browned. It's best to do this in a couple of batches so you don't overcrowd the pan – the chicken pieces need plenty of room around them to brown properly. Remove the chicken and set it aside.

Heat the rest of the oil or ghee in a casserole dish. Add the onion, green chillies and curry leaves and fry them for a few minutes over a high heat. Add the tomatoes and the reserved marinade, then bring everything to the boil. Simmer for a couple of minutes, then add the chicken, skin-side up. Partially cover the pan and simmer for about half an hour, until the chicken is tender and the sauce has reduced. Serve with some rice.

CHICKEN XACUTI

A great sharp coconut-based curry and another Goan favourite, this has a wonderfully complex flavour, thanks to all the spices. We know you'll have to empty your spice cupboard for this but do give it a try. Deseed the chillies if you want to reduce the heat.

SERVES 4

1 chicken, cut into 8 and skinned

juice of ½ lemon

1 tsp turmeric

1 tsp salt

1 tbsp coconut oil

1 onion, sliced

2 green chillies, slit lengthways

2 tbsp tamarind paste

leaves from a bunch of coriander, chopped

MASALA

1 tbsp coconut oil

2 onions, finely chopped

1–2 green chillies

25g root ginger, finely chopped

4 garlic cloves, crushed

½ fresh coconut, grated

stems from a bunch of coriander, chopped

SPICE MIX

1 tbsp coriander seeds

1 tbsp poppy seeds

3cm cinnamon stick

2 star anise

½ tsp black peppercorns

4 cloves

2 tbsp Kashmiri chilli powder (optional)

Put the chicken in a bowl. Mix the lemon juice with the turmeric and salt and pour this over the chicken, then leave it to marinate while you make the masala mixture.

To make the masala, heat the coconut oil in a large frying pan. Add the onions and green chillies and cook for about 5 minutes over a medium heat, stirring regularly. Add the ginger, garlic, coconut and the coriander stems and continue to cook until the coconut looks lightly toasted. Remove the pan from the heat and allow to cool.

For the spice mix, put the whole spices and chilli powder, if using, into a dry frying pan and toast for a couple of minutes until they smell very aromatic. Remove the pan from the heat and transfer the spices to a plate to cool, then grind them to a powder and tip into a bowl.

Blitz the cooled masala mixture to a paste in a food processor, then mix it with the ground spices.

To make the curry, heat the coconut oil in a large frying pan - ideally you want the chicken pieces in one layer while they cook. Cook the onion for several minutes until it's starting to soften, then add the chicken. Fry for a few minutes on each side until browned, then stir in the spicy masala paste, slit green chillies, the tamarind paste, half the coriander leaves and 200ml of water.

Simmer the curry, stirring and turning the pieces over regularly, until the sauce is well reduced and separated - you want it almost dry - and the chicken is cooked through. Garnish with the rest of the coriander leaves and some extra grated coconut if you like.

CHICKEN, LENTIL *and* SPINACH CURRY

This is what happens when we put together two of our favourite curries - chicken dhansak and chicken saag. Could it be a saagsak? Ideal for a midweek supper, this has everything you need in one pot, but some flatbread on the side is good.

SERVES 4

1 tbsp olive oil

1 onion, sliced

4 garlic cloves, finely chopped

small bunch of fresh coriander, stems and leaves separated, finely chopped

1 generous tbsp of medium curry powder

5 skinless, boneless chicken thighs, cut into bite-sized pieces

100g red lentils, well rinsed

600ml chicken stock

400g spinach, washed

juice of ½ lemon

sea salt and freshly ground black pepper

Heat the oil in a large casserole dish or a saucepan. Add the onion and cook it for several minutes until it's starting to soften. Add the garlic, coriander stems and the curry powder and stir to combine. Add the chicken and stir over a medium heat until all the pieces are coated with the spices and seared on all sides.

Add the lentils and the stock or 600ml of water, then season well with salt and pepper. Bring to the boil, then turn the heat down, cover the pan and simmer gently until the lentils are tender and have broken down a little. If the curry starts to look too thick, add a little more water.

Add the spinach, pushing it down into the liquid gradually until it has all wilted. Add the lemon juice, then taste for seasoning. Serve with plenty of finely chopped coriander leaves.

THAI YELLOW CHICKEN CURRY

Fragrant, spicy and flavourful, Thai curries are great favourites of ours. There are quite a few ingredients here, but once you've whizzed up the curry paste the rest doesn't take long – and it'll be well worth it when you take your first mouthful.

SERVES 4

1 tbsp coconut oil

1 onion, sliced

2 Kaffir lime leaves, left whole (optional)

2 skinless, boneless chicken breasts, diced

3 skinless, boneless chicken thighs, diced

2 medium potatoes, cut into chunks

400ml coconut milk

1 tsp palm sugar (or light soft brown sugar)

1 tbsp fish sauce

juice of 1 lime

fresh coriander leaves

CURRY PASTE

4 red shallots, skin on

1 garlic bulb

30g root ginger

2 tsp turmeric

3 lemongrass stems, peeled and chopped

3 tbsp finely chopped fresh coriander stems

4 dried red chillies

1 tbsp ground coriander

1 tsp ground cumin

¼ tsp white pepper

¼ tsp cinnamon

salt

Start with the curry paste. Preheat the oven to 200°C/Fan 180°C/Gas 6. Wrap the shallots, garlic bulb and ginger (unpeeled) in a large sheet of foil and place on a baking tray. Roast them in the oven for about an hour until the shallots and garlic are soft, then set aside to cool.

Peel the cooled shallots and squish the garlic flesh out of the skins. Peel the ginger root. Put everything in a small food processor with the remaining paste ingredients and a generous pinch of salt and grind to a paste – it doesn't have to be completely smooth.

Now for the curry. Heat the coconut oil in a large casserole dish or a saucepan. Add the onion and cook it until slightly softened. Add the curry paste and the Kaffir lime leaves, if using, and fry for a couple of minutes, then stir in the chicken. Cook for several minutes until the chicken is seared and well coated with the curry paste and the paste has started to separate a little.

Add the potatoes, coconut milk and palm sugar. Bring almost to the boil, then turn down the heat and simmer gently until the potatoes are just tender – add a little water if the curry starts to look too dry. Taste, add the fish sauce and then the lime juice, a teaspoon at a time until you think the flavour is right. Add a little salt too if you think the curry needs it.

Serve with jasmine rice and plenty of fresh coriander leaves.

GUNPOWDER CHICKEN

The proper name for this is 'kung pao chicken' and it comes from the Szechuan region of China. The Szechuan peppercorns and chillies really do make this an explosive dish and you can cut them down or ramp them up according to how hot you want to go. Boom!

SERVES 4

500g skinless, boneless chicken thighs, trimmed and diced

1 tsp salt

1 tbsp Szechuan peppercorns

2 tbsp groundnut oil

8 Szechuan chillies, thickly sliced

4 spring onions, sliced into 2cm rounds

2 tbsp roasted peanuts

SAUCE

2 tbsp soy sauce

2 tbsp rice wine

2 tbsp rice vinegar (Chinese black if you can get it)

100ml chicken stock

2 tsp cornflour, mixed with 1 tbsp water

1 tsp caster sugar or honey

Put the diced chicken in a bowl and sprinkle it with the salt. Grind the Szechuan peppercorns finely, then sprinkle a teaspoon of the ground peppercorns over the chicken. Leave the chicken to stand for half an hour or so.

Mix the ingredients for the sauce together so it is ready to use as soon as you need it.

Heat the oil in a wok. When it is hot and shimmering, add the chillies and stir-fry until they turn black. By this time they will have flavoured the oil and you can take them out or leave them in, depending how much heat you can handle.

Add the chicken, spring onions and peanuts. Fry quickly for a minute to brown the chicken, then pour over the sauce, along with the reserved ground Szechuan peppercorns. Turn the heat down and let the chicken cook gently for a few minutes until the sauce is reduced and syrupy.

Serve immediately with some steamed rice.

CARIBBEAN CHICKEN CURRY

Transport yourself to the sunny Caribbean with this carnival of a curry. The potato is traditional, but you could swap it for squash, pumpkin or sweet potato. The spice mix is incredible but if you prefer, you can use two tablespoons of medium curry powder instead.

SERVES 4

1kg chicken drumsticks and thighs, skin on and bone in

juice of 1 lime

1 scotch bonnet chilli, deseeded and finely chopped

2 garlic cloves, crushed or grated

25g root ginger, grated

3 sprigs of thyme

2 bay leaves, crumbled

2 tbsp of the spice mix

2 tbsp coconut oil

1 large onion, sliced

300ml chicken stock

50g creamed coconut

1 potato, diced

1 tbsp rum or brandy

salt and black pepper

SPICE MIX

2 tbsp coriander seeds

1 tbsp cumin seeds

1 tbsp mustard seeds

2 tsp fenugreek seeds

1cm cinnamon stick

1 clove

½ tsp allspice berries

2 tbsp turmeric

1 tbsp garlic powder

Put the chicken in a bowl and season it with salt and pepper. Add the lime juice, scotch bonnet, garlic, ginger, thyme, bay leaves and 2 tablespoons of the spice mix (or curry powder). Stir to coat or get in there with your hands and rub everything into the chicken. Be careful, though, because of the scotch bonnet and wash your hands extra well afterwards. Set the chicken aside for at least an hour, but preferably overnight.

Heat the oil in a large casserole dish. Add the onion and cook for several minutes until it's starting to soften. Add the chicken pieces and stir until the chicken is lightly browned – you might need to do this in a couple of batches. Once all the chicken is browned, pile it all back into the casserole dish and stir.

Pour over the stock and stir in the creamed coconut. Leave to cook, covered, over a low heat for about 45 minutes, adding the potato about half way through. You can add a little water if the curry starts to get too dry. By the end of the cooking time the chicken should be falling off the bone. When the chicken is cooked through, stir in the rum or brandy and simmer for a few more minutes.

SPICE MIX

To make the spice mix, toast the whole spices in a frying pan until they smell aromatic. Transfer them to a plate to cool, then grind them to a fine powder. Mix with the turmeric and garlic powder. You'll have more mix than you need for this dish, but it will keep well in a jar for a few months.

AFRICAN PEANUT *and* CHICKEN STEW

We're used to chicken satay with its peanut sauce and this takes that fantastic combo a stage further. It's a good hearty stew and a great one-pot dish. If you don't want to use a whole chicken, buy some skin-on, bone-in thighs and legs instead.

SERVES 4

1 tbsp groundnut or coconut oil

1 chicken, cut into 8–10 pieces

1 onion, sliced

1 green pepper, deseeded and cut into strips

1 red pepper, deseeded and cut into strips

3 garlic cloves, finely chopped

15g root ginger, finely chopped

1 tbsp ground coriander

2 tsp ground cumin

1 tsp red chilli powder or cayenne

1 tsp dried thyme

1 large sweet potato, cut into chunks

200g smooth peanut butter

600ml chicken stock

100g roasted peanuts

100g okra, sliced (optional)

fresh coriander, chopped

sea salt and freshly ground black pepper

Heat the oil in a large flameproof casserole dish or a saucepan. Season the chicken with salt and pepper, then add it to the pan, skin-side down. Fry until the chicken is a rich golden brown and much of the fat has rendered out, then turn the pieces over and brown them briefly on the other side – you might need to do this in batches. Remove the chicken from the dish and set it aside.

Add the onion and peppers. Fry them over a high heat for a couple of minutes, then add the garlic, ginger, spices, thyme and sweet potato. Cook for another couple of minutes over a medium heat. Whisk the peanut butter with the stock in a bowl until smooth, then add this to the casserole dish together with the peanuts.

Return the chicken to the casserole dish, skin-side up. Simmer for about 15 minutes, uncovered, then add the okra, if using. Simmer for another 15-20 minutes until the chicken is cooked through and the vegetables are tender. Serve garnished with lots of fresh coriander.

LORENZO'S CARIBBEAN JERK CHICKEN

We met Lorenzo Richards at his Wildmoor Oak restaurant in Worcestershire where he serves up Caribbean and international dishes, including his great jerk chicken. Lorenzo wants to spread the word about Caribbean food and he gave us this recipe to share with you. We have adapted it slightly for you to cook at home.

SERVES 6

6 chicken breasts, bone in and skin on

juice of ½ lemon

JERK SEASONING

1 large onion, roughly chopped

5 garlic cloves, crushed

2 tsp grated root ginger

2 spring onions, roughly chopped

½ small scotch bonnet, roughly chopped

leaves from 4 sprigs of thyme

½ tsp curry powder

2 tsp smoked paprika

1 tsp ground cinnamon

2 tsp all-purpose seasoning

70ml soy sauce

150ml vegetable oil

125ml Caribbean barbecue sauce

Put the chicken breasts in a bowl, rub them all over with the lemon juice, then set them aside.

Place the onion, garlic, ginger, spring onions, scotch bonnet, thyme leaves, curry powder, smoked paprika, cinnamon, all-purpose seasoning and soy sauce in a blender and whizz until roughly chopped. With the motor running, slowly pour in the vegetable oil. Stir in the barbecue sauce and your jerk seasoning is now ready.

Pour the jerk seasoning over the chicken breasts, then cover and leave in the fridge to marinate for at least an hour or overnight.

When you're ready to cook the chicken, heat the oven to 210°C/Fan 190°C/Gas 6½. Put the chicken pieces on a foil-lined baking tray and pour over any excess marinade. Cook them for 40 minutes, basting half way through cooking, until the marinade has separated slightly and the chicken is cooked. Baste the chicken one last time, remove it from the oven and leave it to rest for 5 minutes before eating.

Alternatively you can cook the chicken on a barbecue, turning it regularly. Set aside a quarter of the jerk seasoning before marinating for basting the chicken as it cooks. Great with salad, coleslaw and rice.

MINCED *and* CHOPPED CHICKEN

CHICKEN BURGERS

These are a refreshing change from the usual beef, and healthy too. If you don't want to chop the chicken yourself, you could ask your butcher to mince it coarsely for you. It's important to include some of the chicken fat in the mix to keep the burgers nice and juicy.

SERVES 4

500g boneless, skinless chicken thighs

1 small onion, very finely chopped

a few sprigs of tarragon, finely chopped (optional)

1 tsp dried oregano

olive oil

4 burger buns, cut in half

1 tbsp mayonnaise (see page 354)

1 tbsp mustard

lettuce leaves

1 large tomato, sliced

sea salt and freshly ground black pepper

Make sure the chicken thighs are well chilled, or even partially frozen, as this will make them much easier to chop. Using a very sharp knife, dice the chicken as finely as possible, making sure you include any fat that's attached to the thighs. To check you have chopped the chicken finely enough, squeeze some of it together in your hand – it should clump into a ball quite easily.

Put the chicken into a bowl and add the onion, some of the tarragon, if using, and the oregano. Add half a teaspoon of salt and some pepper, then mix it all together well. Divide the chicken into 4 portions and shape into burgers about 2cm thick.

Heat a large griddle or a frying pan to medium hot. Brush the burgers with a little oil, then place them on the griddle or pan, spaced well apart if possible. Leave them to cook for 4 minutes, without moving them, then carefully lift them off with a metal spatula and turn them over. The burgers should be well seared and lift off easily; if they don't, leave them for a little longer. Cook them on the other side for 4 minutes, then carefully flip them over again and cook for another minute on each side or until the meat is no longer pink.

Once the burgers are cooked through, remove them from the griddle or pan and set them aside to rest for a couple of minutes. Toast the cut side of the burger buns very lightly. Whisk the mayonnaise with the mustard and stir in the rest of the tarragon, if using. Spread this on one side of the buns. Add the burgers with lettuce and slices of tomato.

If you like, you can add more herbs or some chilli or citrus zest to your burger mix. Or keep the burgers plain and add a rasher or two of bacon or some avocado slices or even some creamy blue cheese. The possibilities are endless.

CHICKEN MEATLOAF

This is a free-form meatloaf and a dish you will want to cook again and again. Instead of being cooked in a tin, the meatloaf is shaped on a baking tray and the result looks very handsome. A mixture of thighs and breast is good for the mince. Good with some mash and greens – yum, yum.

SERVES 4

1 tbsp olive oil

1 small onion, finely chopped

2 garlic cloves, crushed

750g chicken mince

50g streaky bacon, finely chopped

1 tsp ground oregano

1 tsp lemon zest

1 tsp Dijon mustard

1 tsp Worcestershire sauce

50ml double cream

100g breadcrumbs

2 egg whites

100g Gruyère cheese, grated

5 rashers of rindless streaky bacon

sea salt and freshly ground black pepper

GLAZE

100ml tomato ketchup

1 tsp Worcestershire sauce

1 tbsp Dijon mustard

1 tbsp maple syrup

1 tbsp cider vinegar

Preheat the oven to 180°C/Fan 160°C/Gas 4. Heat the olive oil in a frying pan. Add the onion and fry it gently for a few minutes until soft and starting to take on some colour. Add the garlic and cook for a further minute, then remove the pan from the heat and leave the onion and garlic to cool.

Put the chicken mince in a large bowl and season it with salt and pepper. Add the chopped bacon, oregano, lemon zest, Dijon mustard, Worcestershire sauce, double cream and breadcrumbs, followed by the cooled onion and garlic. Add the egg whites and stir well. Take a small piece of the mixture and fry it. Taste, then adjust the seasoning and any other flavours until you're happy.

To make the glaze, put all the ingredients into a saucepan and season with salt and pepper. Heat through gently, then set aside.

Take half the meatloaf mixture, and mould it into a loaf shape on a baking tray. Use the size of a loaf pan for guidance and make the shape as even as you can. Put the cheese down the centre, making sure you leave a border all the way round, then top with the remaining mixture. Build it up around the sides and make sure it is well sealed as you don't want the cheese leaking out. You should end up with a slightly domed loaf. Brush it with some of the glaze.

Cut the bacon rashers in half and stretch them with the back of a knife. They need to be long enough to reach from the base of one side of the loaf, over the top and to the bottom of the other side. Place the rashers side by side over the loaf until it is completely covered – except for each end. Brush with a little more of the glaze.

Bake the meatloaf for 30 minutes, then remove it and brush with the remaining glaze. Bake for a further 30 minutes, by which time the meatloaf should be cooked through with nicely browned bacon. Serve in thick slices.

CHICKEN *and* MOZZARELLA MEATBALLS

We cooked these meatballs with their little hidden surprises on 'Saturday Kitchen' and they went down a storm. The sauce is a bit special too because you include some oven-roasted tomatoes with the canned, which gives loads of extra depth to the flavour.

SERVES 4

750g chicken mince, half breast, half thigh

2 tbsp olive oil

1 small onion, finely chopped

1 garlic clove, finely chopped

1 tsp dried oregano

50g breadcrumbs

1 egg, beaten

50ml double cream

30g Parmesan cheese, finely grated, plus extra for topping

grating of nutmeg

20 mini mozzarella balls, plus extra for topping

20 basil leaves

200g pappardelle

sea salt and freshly ground black pepper

TOMATO SAUCE

3 tbsp olive oil

2 tbsp balsamic vinegar

500g fresh plum tomatoes

1 onion, chopped

2 garlic cloves

1 tsp dried oregano

100ml red wine

400g can of tomatoes

pinch of sugar

First start the tomato sauce. Preheat the oven to 200°C/Fan 180°C/Gas 6. Add 2 tablespoons of olive oil and the balsamic vinegar to a roasting tin and season with salt and pepper. Cut the fresh tomatoes in half, add them to the tin and coat them in the oil and vinegar mixture. Roast for about 30 minutes until soft and unctuous.

Meanwhile heat the remaining olive oil in a large saucepan, add the onion and fry it gently until very soft and translucent. Add the garlic and oregano and cook for a further minute, then pour in the wine. Allow the wine to bubble up for a minute or so, then turn down the heat and add the canned tomatoes. Season with salt and pepper.

Cover the pan and leave the sauce to simmer for as long as you can, but for at least an hour. Check it regularly and add a splash of water if it appears to be getting dry. After the first 20 minutes, check the tomatoes for sweetness and add a pinch of sugar if you think they need it. When the roasted tomatoes are ready, put them in a sieve and press them through the sieve into the pan of sauce to extract every bit of flavour.

To make the meatballs, put the mince in a large bowl and season with salt and pepper. Heat a tablespoon of oil in a small frying pan and add the onion. Fry gently until very soft and translucent, then add the garlic and cook for a further minute. Cool the onion and garlic slightly, add them to the chicken, then add the oregano, breadcrumbs, egg, cream, cheese and nutmeg. Mix thoroughly, then divide the mixture into 20 balls.

Flatten each meatball. Thoroughly drain the mozzarella balls, wrap each one in a basil leaf and put it in the middle of a meatball. Wrap the meat around the mozzarella and basil until it is completely enclosed. Shape gently into a sphere. Repeat with the remaining meatballs.

Heat another tablespoon of oil in a large frying pan and fry the meatballs on each side until well browned. Or if you prefer, you can bake the meatballs instead. Just put them on a baking tray and bake for 10 minutes at 220°C/Fan 200°C/Gas 7.

Preheat the oven to 200°C/Fan 180°C/Gas 6 (or turn it down if you have baked the meatballs). Once the meatballs are cooked, transfer them to an ovenproof dish and pour over the tomato sauce – it won't completely cover them but that's fine. Slice any extra mozzarella you have and arrange it over the sauce, then sprinkle some more Parmesan on top. Bake in the preheated oven for 20–25 minutes until piping hot.

While the meatballs are baking, cook the pasta in a large saucepan of boiling water according to the packet instructions. Serve it with the meatballs and sauce. Offer more grated Parmesan if you like.

PULLED CHICKEN *with coleslaw*

Everyone loves pulled pork so about trying pulled chicken for a change? It's totally superb and is great served warm in rolls or baguette with some coleslaw. This makes excellent sandwiches too so just right for a special picnic.

SERVES 4

750g chicken thighs, bone in, but skinned

sea salt and freshly ground black pepper

BARBECUE SAUCE

1 tbsp olive oil

1 large onion, finely chopped

3 garlic cloves, tfinely chopped

1 tsp oregano

1 tsp smoked paprika

1 tsp cumin

1 tbsp tomato purée

400g can of tomatoes

1 tbsp maple syrup

1 tbsp cider vinegar

1 tbsp soy sauce

1 tsp Dijon mustard

1 tsp Worcestershire sauce

1 tsp hot sauce (optional)

200ml beer (light ale or lager)

First make the barbecue sauce. Heat the oil in a saucepan. Add the onion and fry it gently over a medium heat until softened and slightly browned. Add the garlic, oregano and spices and stir for a further minute, then stir in the tomato purée. Season with salt and pepper and stir until the paste starts to separate. Add all the other sauce ingredients, except the beer, then simmer for 15 minutes to allow the flavours to blend and the sauce to reduce a little. Tip the sauce into a blender and blitz until smooth, then mix it with the beer.

Preheat the oven to 150°C/Fan 30°C/Gas 2. Put the chicken in a large flameproof casserole dish and season it with salt and pepper. Pour over the sauce and beer mixture and bring it to the boil, then cover the casserole dish tightly with a lid or with foil.

Cook the chicken in the oven for an hour and a half, checking it after an hour. When the chicken is ready, the meat will fall off the bones and pull apart easily.

Remove the chicken from the sauce and set it aside. Put the pan of sauce back on the hob and simmer to reduce it a little – it should be quite loose, the consistency of a tomato sauce for pasta.

Using a couple of forks, shred the chicken, discarding any bones or tendons. Put the chicken back in the sauce and keep it warm. Serve the chicken with coleslaw and soft rolls.

COLESLAW

½ white cabbage, finely shredded

1 small onion, finely chopped

1 large carrot, cut into matchsticks or grated

1 celery stick, finely chopped

1 tsp sugar

1 tsp cider vinegar

1 tbsp mayonnaise

1 tbsp crème fraiche

1 tsp lime zest

1 tsp lime juice

2 tbsp dill, finely chopped

To make the coleslaw, put all the vegetables in a colander and sprinkle them with salt and the sugar and vinegar. Leave the vegetables to stand for an hour to rid them of any excess water. Transfer them to a large bowl.

Whisk the mayonnaise with crème fraiche and add the lime zest and lime juice. Mix this into the vegetables, then stir in the dill.

CHICKEN FAJITAS

We love this kind of food. You pile everything on the table and let everyone help themselves to what they want. Great with a jug of frozen margaritas for a party.

SERVES 4

600g skinless, boneless chicken breasts or thighs, cut into strips

2 tbsp olive oil

2 red onions, cut into wedges

2 red peppers, deseeded and sliced

1 green pepper, deseeded and sliced

MARINADE

juice of 2 limes

1 tsp ground cumin

1 tsp ground coriander

1 tsp garlic powder

1 tsp dried oregano

2 tsp chipotle paste

1 tbsp tomato purée

1 tbsp soy sauce

4 garlic cloves, crushed

sea salt and freshly ground black pepper

TO SERVE

guacamole (see p.361)

8 flour tortillas, warmed through

100g grated cheese

200g soured cream

Mix together the marinade ingredients in a large bowl and season with salt and pepper. Add the chicken to the bowl, mix well and leave it to stand for at least half an hour.

Heat the oil in a frying pan. Add the red onions and peppers and fry them over a medium heat for just a few minutes until they have started to soften but still have a little bite to them. Add the chicken to the pan and continue to fry until the chicken is cooked through.

Prepare all the side dishes. For the guacamole, see page 361. Serve everything separately at the table so everyone can assemble their own fajitas.

CHICKEN *and* PORK TERRINE

We like the mix of belly pork and shoulder in this, but if you prefer you could just use pork mince from the butcher. This is a cracking little number and makes a fab starter for a special meal or to serve for lunch with a salad. And, of course, it's just the thing for a picnic.

SERVES 4

CHICKEN LAYER

400g skinless, boneless chicken breasts

100ml white wine

zest of 1 lemon

leaves from a sprig of thyme

1 tbsp olive oil

4 tbsp finely chopped parsley

sea salt and freshly ground black pepper

PORK LAYERS

300g trimmed pork shoulder

300g rindless pork belly

zest of 1 lemon

1 tbsp finely chopped thyme leaves

¼ tsp ground ginger

75g dried apricots, soaked in warm water if necessary

25g pistachio kernels, halved

TO ASSEMBLE

400g rindless streaky bacon rashers

First marinate the chicken. Slice the breasts into strips, put them in a bowl and season with salt and pepper. Add the wine, zest and thyme leaves, then drizzle over the oil. Cover and marinate for at least an hour.

Finely chop the pork shoulder and belly, or put the whole lot through a meat grinder, or whizz it in a food processor. Then put the pork in a bowl, season with salt and pepper and add the lemon zest, thyme leaves and ground ginger. Finely chop the apricots and mix them and the pistachios into the pork.

Preheat the oven to 150°C/Fan 130°C/Gas 2. Put the bacon rashers on a board and stretch them with the back of a knife. Use the rashers to line a 1.2-litre terrine mould, arranging them widthways and placing them so they criss-cross and slightly overlap each other. The bacon rashers should overlap the mould by about 5cm on each side. If they don't, stretch them a little more.

Put half the pork mixture into the terrine and spread it out evenly. Mix the chicken with the finely chopped parsley, then lay the strips out in an even layer over the pork. Finally, cover with the remaining pork. Cover the top of the terrine with the overhanging bacon slices, continuing with the criss-cross arrangement, then top with more slices so the filling is covered.

Put the lid on the terrine or cover it with a double layer of foil. Put the terrine in a roasting tin and add enough just-boiled water to reach about 2cm up the sides. Put the tin in the oven and bake the terrine for 1 hour and 30 minutes. To check the terrine is cooked, test it with a meat thermometer or probe – it should be 75°C. Alternatively, hold a skewer in the centre for a few seconds – if the tip is too hot to touch for more than a second, the terrine is done.

Cover the terrine with a couple of layers of foil, then weigh it down with something heavy such as a couple of tins. Leave it to cool, then chill overnight in the fridge. To serve, turn the terrine out and slice.

CHICKEN LIVER PÂTÉ

This is a brilliant pâté and served on toast with some little cornichons and onions it's almost a meal in itself. It's great to have in the fridge to pick at when the hunger pangs strike – one of those things that you wonder why you don't have more often.

SERVES 6

50g butter

1 onion, finely chopped

leaves from a sprig of thyme, finely chopped

a few white peppercorns, finely crushed

a few juniper berries, crushed

pinch of ground ginger

400g chicken livers, cleaned and roughly chopped

50ml brandy or any type of eau de vie,

25ml Madeira or Marsala

75ml double cream

TOPPING

250ml apple juice

1 tsp juniper berries, crushed

sprig of thyme

50ml Madeira

3 gelatine leaves

Melt 10-15g of the butter in a large frying pan. When the butter has melted, add the onion and cook it gently until it has softened and is completely translucent.

Add the thyme and spices, then turn up the heat a little and add the chicken livers. Sauté them for 2 or 3 minutes until they're seared on all sides and pink, rather than red, in the middle. Make sure they still have some 'bounce' or give.

Transfer the contents of the frying pan to a food processor. Put the pan back on the hob, turn up the heat and pour in the brandy. Set light to it, wait for it to burn off, then add the Madeira or Marsala and reduce it to just 2-3 tablespoons. Pour this into the food processor and add the double cream. Blitz everything together until smooth, then add the rest of the butter and blitz again. If you want a very smooth pâté, push the whole lot through a sieve.

Put the mixture into a dish and spread it evenly. Leave it to cool.

For the topping, heat the apple juice in a small saucepan with the juniper berries and thyme. Simmer until the juice has reduced by half, then add the Madeira and simmer for another minute.

Soak the gelatine leaves in cold water until soft, then wring them out and add them to the pan. Stir over a very low heat (do not let it boil), until the gelatine has melted, then strain. Allow the mixture to cool very slightly, then pour it over the pâté. Leave it in the fridge to set. Serve with toast and some gherkins and cocktail onions.

JAPANESE CHICKEN MEATBALLS

Teriyaki sauces are often either really sweet, with lots of added sugar, or too salty, so we've come up with a version that we think is light but still tasty and savoury enough to go well with the meatballs. You will yen for another helping.

SERVES 4

25g dried shiitake mushrooms

600g minced chicken

100g breadcrumbs

1 large shallot, finely chopped

10g root ginger, finely chopped

1 garlic clove, finely chopped

1 tbsp fresh coriander stems, finely chopped

1 tbsp soy sauce

1 egg white

1 tbsp sesame seeds, to serve

a few shredded spring onions, to serve

sea salt and freshly ground black pepper

TERIYAKI SAUCE

150ml light soy sauce

50ml dark soy sauce

150ml mirin

1 tbsp rice vinegar

1 tsp honey

1 garlic clove, crushed

20g root ginger, grated

1 tsp chilli flakes (optional)

Soak the dried mushrooms in a bowl of warm water for 30 minutes.

Drain the soaked mushrooms and chop them finely, then put them in a bowl with the minced chicken and all the other meatball ingredients, except the sesame seeds and spring onions. Season with salt and pepper, then mix thoroughly. If the mixture seems too loose, add more breadcrumbs. Put the mixture in the fridge to chill for half an hour. Preheat the oven to 200°C/Fan 180°C/Gas 6.

Form the mixture into balls, each about 30g – you should have about 24. Mould them around flat bamboo skewers, putting about 3 on each skewer. Put the skewers on a baking tray and bake the meatballs in the oven for 10–12 minutes until just cooked through.

To make the sauce, put the soy sauces, mirin, rice vinegar, honey, garlic, ginger and chilli flakes, if using, in a small saucepan with 50ml of water. Bring to the boil and simmer for about 10 minutes until the liquid is reduced and syrupy. Make sure the sauce isn't too thick, as it will reduce further when it is cooked with the meatballs.

Put the baked meatballs in a large frying pan and ladle over some of the sauce. Heat them gently, turning the skewers so the meatballs are completely covered in the sauce. When they are glossy, remove them from the frying pan. Put them on a serving plate and sprinkle over the sesame seeds and shredded spring onions.

Serve with more of the sauce on the side for dipping and some steamed rice if you like.

CHILLI CHICKEN

Tomatillos are the traditional Mexican ingredient but if you've got a glut of green tomatoes in the garden this is a great way to use them up. Alternatively, you could add red tomatoes or 400ml of coconut milk instead. You can find curd cheese at the cheese counter in many supermarkets but if you don't have any, just leave it out. No problem.

SERVES 4

1 tbsp oil

1 onion, finely chopped

1 green pepper, deseeded and diced

2 celery sticks, finely chopped

3 garlic cloves, finely chopped

2 jalapeño chillies, deseeded and finely chopped

1 tsp ground cumin

1 tsp ground coriander

pinch of cinnamon

bunch of coriander, stems and leaves separated and chopped

600g chicken mince

500g green tomatoes or tomatillos, cored and puréed

zest and juice of 1 lime

½ tsp sugar

salt and pepper

TO SERVE

1 avocado, flesh diced

1 jalapeño chilli, deseeded and diced

1 red tomato, diced

juice of ½ lime

50g curd cheese, crumbled (optional)

Heat the oil in a large flameproof casserole dish or a saucepan. Add the onion, pepper and celery and sauté for several minutes over a low to medium heat until they're soft and translucent, then add the garlic, chillies, spices and coriander stems. Cook for a further 2-3 minutes, then add the chicken and season well with salt and pepper.

Turn up the heat and cook briskly until the chicken is lightly browned, then add the tomatoes or tomatillos (or the coconut milk, if using), the lime zest, sugar and a splash of water. Simmer the chilli for 15-20 minutes, uncovered, checking every so often to make sure the sauce isn't getting too dry.

Taste to check the seasoning and add the lime juice and half of the coriander leaves.

Mix the rest of the coriander leaves with the avocado, jalapeño, diced red tomato and lime juice and serve with the chilli, grilled tortillas or rice and the crumbled cheese, if using.

CHOPPED LIVER

To make this a really authentic Jewish dish, include the schmaltz and gribenes. Schmaltz is rendered chicken fat, made by cooking chicken skin until crispy. These tasty little nuggets of crispy skin are called gribenes and are naughty but oh so nice.

SERVES 4

1 tbsp schmaltz and 15g butter or 30g butter

1 large onion, finely chopped

400g chicken livers, trimmed, rinsed and patted dry

pinch of cayenne

2 tbsp gribenes, finely chopped (optional)

3 hard-boiled eggs, whites and yolks separated

2 tbsp brandy

2 tbsp finely chopped parsley

sea salt and freshly ground black pepper

SCHMALTZ AND GRIBENES

skin from 2 chicken thighs

salt

If you're making the schmaltz and gribenes, preheat the oven to 200°C/ Fan 180°C/Gas 6. Put the chicken skin in a small roasting dish and sprinkle it with salt. Roast in the oven for 25–30 minutes, by which time the skin should be crisp and brown, and plenty of fat should have rendered out into the pan. Drain the chicken skin on kitchen paper and when it's cool enough, chop it into crisp little nuggets. Pour the fat (schmaltz) into a bowl.

Put the schmaltz and/or the butter into a frying pan. Heat until the butter has melted, then add the onion. Cook very gently until it's soft and translucent, then turn up the heat a little and let the onion brown very lightly. Push the onion to one side and add the chicken livers. Cook them for about 3 minutes on each side, until well browned but still bouncy. Season with salt, pepper and cayenne.

Remove the pan from the heat and leave the livers to cool. Tip them into a food processor and pulse until you have a coarse-textured pâté. Tip it into a bowl and add the gribenes, if you've made some. Finely chop the egg whites and the yolks. Reserve 2 tablespoons of whites and 1 tablespoon of yolks for the garnish, then mix all the rest with the chicken livers. Pour over the brandy and mix again, then smooth out the top.

Sprinkle over the reserved egg whites, followed by the yolks and finally top with chopped parsley. Serve with crackers and perhaps some cornichons on the side.

SPICY CHICKEN *on* LETTUCE

These little parcels of tastiness are a version of laab, a Southeast Asian minced meat salad, but with Middle Eastern flavours this time. They make a lovely snack or light lunch. By the way, sumac is a spice with a tangy lemony flavour and well worth having in your cupboard.

SERVES 4

1 tbsp olive oil

300g boneless, skinless chicken thighs, minced or finely chopped

1 garlic clove, finely chopped

1 tsp ground cumin

1 tsp ground coriander

¼ tsp ground cinnamon

¼ tsp ground ginger

pinch of ground cloves

pinch of cayenne

juice of 1 lemon

50ml chicken stock

1 tsp honey

sea salt and freshly ground black pepper

TO SERVE

2 or 3 little gem lettuces, leaves separated

½ small red onion, finely diced

2 tbsp each of finely fresh chopped coriander, mint and parsley

sumac, for dusting

Heat the olive oil in a frying pan. Add the chicken and fry it over a high heat for a couple of minutes until it's lightly cooked. Add the garlic, then sprinkle in all the spices and season with salt and pepper.

Pour in the lemon juice and the chicken stock, then stir in the honey. Simmer until the sauce has reduced to just about nothing – the mixture needs to be quite dry. Remove the pan from the heat and set it aside to cool a little.

To serve, pile the chicken mixture on to little gem leaves. Mix the onion and herbs together as a garnish and sprinkle them over the chicken. Finally, dust with a little sumac and serve immediately.

CHINESE STEAMED CHICKEN MEATBALLS

You want meatballs? We've got lots, and these show just how versatile chicken can be. They're great as part of a dim sum feast or as a starter. Chinese supermarkets sell black bean paste but if you don't have any, peanut butter makes a good substitute.

SERVES 4

600g minced chicken

1 tsp Chinese five-spice

4 spring onions, finely chopped

50g water chestnuts, finely chopped

4 tbsp finely chopped fresh coriander leaves

1 red chilli, chopped

1 garlic clove, finely chopped

5g root ginger, grated

1 tbsp soy sauce

1 tsp finely grated orange zest (optional)

100g panko breadcrumbs

1 egg white

sesame oil, for brushing

sea salt and freshly ground black pepper

HOISIN SAUCE

1–2 tbsp black bean paste or peanut butter

2 tbsp dark soy sauce

2 tbsp light soy sauce

1 tbsp brown sugar

1 tsp Chinese five-spice

1 garlic clove, crushed

2 tsp rice wine vinegar

1 tsp sesame oil

1–2 tsp hot sauce

Put the chicken in a bowl and season it with salt and pepper. Sprinkle over the Chinese five-spice, then add all the remaining ingredients, except the sesame oil. Mix thoroughly.

Form the mixture into balls of 40-50g each – you should get about 16-20. Chill the balls for at least 15 minutes or until you are ready to cook them.

Arrange the balls in a steamer. They shouldn't be touching each other so it's best to cook them in a couple of batches. Brush them sparingly with sesame oil, then steam them for 15-20 minutes until they are completely cooked through.

To make the hoisin sauce, put all the ingredients into a bowl, starting with just a tablespoon of black bean paste or peanut butter, and whisk together or blitz in a food processor until fairly smooth. Taste and add more black bean paste if necessary, a teaspoon at a time.

Serve the meatballs with the sauce and some freshly cooked greens.

For an extra chilli whammy, put 50ml of soy sauce in a bowl and add a sliced red chilli.

CHICKEN CROQUETTES

There's something totally irresistible about croquettes. If you don't fancy deep-frying, you can also bake these in a hot oven. To bake the croquettes, put them on a baking tray, drizzle or spray them with oil and cook them in a hot oven – 220°C/Fan 200°C/Gas 7 – for 15-20 minutes.

MAKES 30

700ml whole milk

1 small onion

3 cloves

1 bay leaf

1 tsp black peppercorns

1 tbsp olive oil

75g butter

1 onion, very finely chopped

200g plain flour

200g cooked chicken, finely chopped

1 tbsp finely chopped parsley

2 eggs

150g fine breadcrumbs

vegetable oil, for brushing and deep-frying

sea salt and freshly ground black pepper

Put the milk in a saucepan. Stud the onion with the cloves and add it to the milk with the bay leaf and peppercorns. Heat the milk to just below boiling point, then remove the pan from the heat and leave the milk to infuse until cool. Strain the milk, discarding the aromatics and any skin.

While the milk is cooling, make the roux. Heat the oil and butter in a saucepan. When the butter has melted, add the onion with a pinch of salt and sauté very gently until soft and translucent. Stir in 100g of the flour and keep stirring for a couple of minutes to cook. Start incorporating the milk, a little at a time, stirring after every addition. Season with salt and pepper, then mix in the chicken and parsley.

Line a roasting tin with cling film and brush it with oil. Spread the croquette mix over evenly – it should be about 2.5cm thick. Cover it with another sheet of oiled cling film. When the mixture has cooled, put it in the fridge and leave it for several hours, but preferably overnight. When you're ready to cook the croquettes, remove the mixture from the dish, using the cling film to transfer it to a flat surface. Cut the mixture into 30 even strips.

Put 50g of the remaining flour in a shallow bowl, beat one of the eggs in another, and half the breadcrumbs into a third bowl. Take each strip of croquette and shape it into a sausage. Dip it in the flour, dust off any excess, then dip it in the egg. Finally, roll it in the breadcrumbs. Replenish the flour, egg and breadcrumbs half way through making your croquettes so things don't get too messy.

Chill the croquettes again just to firm them up a little. You can also freeze them at this stage. To cook, half fill a deep fryer or saucepan with oil and heat to 180°C. If you don't have a thermometer, test the oil by adding a cube of bread – it should turn brown in 30 seconds. Fry the croquettes a few at a time – don't overcrowd the pan – for 3-4 minutes until they are a rich golden brown. Drain them on kitchen paper and serve hot.

CHICKEN TACOS

You can buy tortillas to save time but if you fancy making your own, use masa harina – a Mexican flour made with cooked corn kernels. It's gluten free too. You can dress these how you like – hot and spicy or cool and tangy with our salsa and crema; a proper fiesta of a feast.

TORTILLAS

250g masa harina

or 8 ready-made corn tortillas

CHICKEN

1 tbsp olive or coconut oil

2 cooked chicken breasts or 4 chicken thighs, thickly sliced

1 tsp cumin

1 tsp smoked garlic granules

1 tsp dried oregano

sea salt and freshly ground black pepper

TOMATO SALSA

3 large tomatoes, diced

2 chillies (preferably jalapeños), deseeded and finely chopped

1 garlic clove, finely chopped

4 spring onions, finely chopped

juice of 1 lime

1 tbsp tequila (optional)

4 tbsp fresh coriander, finely chopped

If making your tacos from scratch, prepare the tortillas first. Put the masa harina in a bowl and pour in 330ml of hot water. Mix thoroughly with a spoon to start with, then knead with your hands until you have a smooth dough. Make sure the dough isn't too dry – it shouldn't crack easily when you pinch it – and add a little more hot water if necessary. Divide the mixture into 8 pieces and roll each into a ball.

If you have a tortilla press, place some cling film on one side of the press, put a ball in the centre of it, and another piece of cling film on top. Press down firmly. You should have a tortilla about 15cm in diameter. Alternatively, place each ball between 2 sheets of cling film. Put something heavy – such as a cast-iron frying pan – on top, making sure it is centred, and press down as firmly as you can.

Now for the chicken. Heat the oil in a frying pan, add the chicken and sprinkle in the cumin, garlic granules and oregano. Season with salt and pepper. Fry, stirring regularly, until the chicken is heated through, well browned and coated in all the spices.

To make the salsa, mix everything together and season with salt and black pepper.

To make the crema, put the avocado in a blender with the lime juice, sour cream and yoghurt. Season with salt and blitz until smooth.

To assemble, heat a heavy-based frying pan or griddle until it is very hot. Cook each tortilla for 15 seconds on one side, then lift it off – it should come away immediately but if it doesn't it hasn't cooked for quite long enough. Cook it on the other side for 30 seconds. Flip again and cook for a further 15 seconds. Remove and keep warm while you cook the remaining tortillas. If using ready-made tortillas, just warm them through.

Serve the tortillas with the chicken, salsa, crema, lettuce and lime wedges. Some chilli sauce might be good too.

SWEET EGGS

CRÈME CARAMEL

People seem to have forgotten about this dish in recent years, but it is so simple – just a few ingredients – and it makes a tasty end to a meal. You could can also make it in one large ovenproof dish (1.2 litres capacity) and bake it for about one and a half hours.

SERVES 6

butter, for greasing
600ml whole milk
1 vanilla pod, split
2 eggs
4 egg yolks
40g caster sugar

CARAMEL
125g caster sugar

First grease 6 ramekins with butter and set them aside. Put the milk in a saucepan and add the vanilla pod. Heat the milk until it is just about to boil, then remove the pan from the hob and leave the milk to infuse.

To make the caramel, put the sugar in a medium, preferably stainless-steel, saucepan. Give the pan a shake so the sugar spreads evenly over the base, then pour in just enough water to cover the sugar – no more than 75ml. Place the pan over a medium heat.

Keeping stirring to an absolute minimum and just shaking the pan occasionally, gently simmer the sugar and water until the sugar has melted. Continue to cook until it has turned a deep golden brown, but watch it very carefully as the caramel can turn very quickly, and if it gets too dark it will taste bitter. Divide the caramel between the ramekins and swirl, making sure the bases are completely covered. Set aside while you make the custard.

Put the eggs and egg yolks in a bowl with the sugar. Beat until well combined, but not aerated. Reheat the milk until it is about blood temperature, then strain it and pour it steadily over the eggs and sugar, stirring constantly. Leave the custard mixture to stand for a while, then skim off any air bubbles.

Preheat the oven to 150°C/Fan 130°C/Gas 2. Pour the custard into the ramekins and put them in a large roasting tin. Pour in enough just-boiled water to go two-thirds up the sides of the ramekins. Bake in the oven for 25–30 minutes until the custard is set with a slight wobble in the centre.

Let the crème caramels cool down, then chill them for several hours. To serve, run a knife around the edge of each one and turn out on to plates.

HOME-MADE LEMON CURD

This is a childhood favourite and we've been making our own for years. For best results, it's well worth using free-range eggs and unwaxed lemons for this the most luscious of curds. Use it to fill a cake or simply slather it generously on a slice of bread or a toasted crumpet and enjoy.

MAKES 5 JARS

4 eggs

4 egg yolks

200g caster sugar

6 lemons, juice of all 6 and zest of 3

150g unsalted butter, cut into small cubes

Sterilise the jam jars. First wash the jars in soapy water and rinse them in clean warm water. Put them in a low oven (140°C/Fan 120°C/Gas 1) for half an hour to dry completely.

Whisk the eggs and egg yolks in a large heatproof bowl until well combined. Add the sugar and stir in the lemon juice and zest. Add the butter and set the bowl over a saucepan of very gently simmering water, making sure the bottom of the bowl doesn't touch the water.

Stir the mixture with a wooden spoon for 5 minutes until the butter melts, then cook for 10–12 minutes, whisking constantly. The lemon curd should have the consistency of custard and leave a light trail when the whisk is lifted. It will continue to thicken in the jars.

Pour the hot lemon curd into the warmed, sterilised jars and leave to cool. Cover the curd with a disc of waxed paper or baking parchment and seal with a lid. Keep in the fridge and use within 2 weeks.

LEMON CURD CAKE

There's something about a lemon cake. Give us a slice of this and a cuppa and we're happy.
You can buy a nice jar of lemon curd but this cake is extra specially good with our home-made
(see page 312). More tea. Vicar?

────── MAKES 8 SLICES ──────

225g butter, at room
temperature, plus extra
for greasing

225g light soft brown
sugar

zest and juice of
1 lemon

225g plain flour

2 tsp baking powder

4 eggs

2 tbsp milk (if needed)

icing sugar, for dusting

FILLING

200g lemon curd

200ml double or
whipping cream

Preheat the oven to 180°C/Fan 160°C/Gas 4. Grease 2 x 20cm deep
sandwich tins with a little butter and line them with baking parchment,
or spray them with cake release spray.

Beat the butter, sugar and lemon zest in a bowl until very pale, soft and
fluffy. Whisk the flour and baking powder together in a separate bowl.

Add the eggs to the creamed butter and sugar one at a time, following
each with a heaped tablespoon of flour. Once all the eggs are
incorporated, fold in the rest of the flour, then add the lemon juice.
The mixture should have a dropping consistency so add just a little milk
if it is too stiff. If the mixture seems fine, don't add the milk.

Divide the cake batter between the tins and smooth the tops as evenly
as you can. Bake in the oven for about 25 minutes until the cakes have
shrunk away slightly from the sides of the tins and the sponge is springy.
Leave the cakes to cool in the tins for several minutes, then turn them out
on to a cooling rack.

When the cakes are cool, spread the top of one with the lemon curd.
Whip the cream until fairly stiff and pile this over the lemon curd. Place
the other cake on top. Dust the top of the cake with icing sugar.

BANANA CRÈME BRÛLÉE

Bananas and custard bring back memories of childhood for both of us, and this is a rather sophisticated version that brings together a kids' pud with a grown-up crème brûlée. We think that this could be a new Hairy Biker classic.

SERVES 4

25g butter, plus extra for greasing

25g dark brown sugar

pinch of salt

pinch of cinnamon

4 bananas, peeled and sliced diagonally

25ml rum

CUSTARD

600ml double cream

1 vanilla pod, split

6 egg yolks

15g soft light brown sugar

15g soft dark brown sugar

TOPPING

2 tbsp demerara sugar

Grease 4 shallow ramekins with butter and set them aside. Melt the butter in a frying pan and when it starts to foam, add the sugar, salt and cinnamon. Stir until the sugar has melted.

Add the slices of banana and cook them for a couple of minutes on each side until lightly browned. Heat the rum in a small saucepan or a ladle and set it alight, then carefully pour it over the bananas. When the flames subside, divide the bananas between the ramekins.

To make the custard, put the double cream in a saucepan with the vanilla pod. Heat until the cream is almost boiling, then remove the pan from the heat and leave the cream to infuse for 10 minutes. Lightly whisk the egg yolks with the sugar in a bowl, just to combine, then pour the cream over the eggs in a continuous thin stream until all is combined. Rinse out the saucepan and pour everything back into it, including the vanilla pod.

Stir the mixture continuously over a low to medium heat until you have a thick, just pourable custard. Do not leave the custard unattended as it may split. To guard against this, have a bowl of iced water at the ready. If need be, plunge the saucepan into the water, then beat the custard like crazy with a whisk. When the custard is well thickened – this will take at least 10 minutes – pour it over the bananas. When cool, put the ramekins in the fridge to chill, preferably for at least 6 hours.

For the burnt sugar topping, make sure the surface of the custard is completely dry and blot it with kitchen paper if necessary. Sprinkle the sugar over the top, then put the ramekins under a very hot grill or blast them with a blow torch until the sugar is browned and bubbling.

MERINGUES

Whenever you have some leftover egg whites, it's a good excuse to make some meringues and these are heaven on a plate – like crystallised clouds. You can halve this recipe if you don't want to make so many, but when did you ever have too many meringues?

6 egg whites

300g caster sugar

FILLING

300ml double cream

400g strawberries, hulled and quartered

1 tbsp caster sugar

1 tbsp limoncello, or lemon juice

a few sprigs of mint

Preheat the oven to 150°C/Fan 130°C/Gas 2. Line a couple of baking trays with non-stick baking parchment. Using a stand mixer or a hand-held electric mixer, whisk the egg whites to soft peaks.

Add half the sugar to the egg whites, a tablespoon at a time, whisking constantly in between each addition until the mixture forms stiff glossy peaks. Fold in the rest of the sugar as gently as you can.

Put tiny blobs of the meringue in the corners of the baking parchment to help it stick to the baking trays, then pile on the mixture, free form, to make 12 large meringues.

Bake them in the preheated oven for 15 minutes, then turn the oven down to 120°C/Fan 100°C/Gas ½. Continue to bake for 1 hour, until the meringues are very dry and easily lift off the baking tray. Turn off the oven and leave the meringues inside to cool down, then transfer them to an airtight container until needed.

To fill, whip the cream and chill it well. Put the strawberries in a bowl and sprinkle them with the sugar and either the limoncello or lemon juice, then leave them to macerate for about half an hour.

Strain off the liquid from the strawberries if it is excessive – this will depend on how watery they are – and fold them into the cream. Spoon the mixture on to the meringues or serve alongside. Garnish with a few sprigs of mint.

MACARONS

These are so fashionable at the moment and very posh, but we think you can be just as posh in Peterborough as in Paris. Yes, they are a bit fiddly, but if we can do it so can you.

MAKES 20

140g icing sugar

90g ground almonds

2 large egg whites

20g caster sugar

BUTTERCREAM FILLING

100g butter

1 tbsp orange marmalade, any peel very finely chopped or taken out

1 tsp orange zest

½ tsp orange blossom water

50g icing sugar

Preheat the oven to 150°C/Fan 130°C/Gas 2. Take 2 pieces of baking parchment and draw 20 x 3cm diameter circles on each piece.

Blitz the icing sugar and ground almonds together in a food processor, then sieve them into a large bowl. Whisk the egg whites to stiff peaks stage with a hand-held mixer, then gradually incorporate the caster sugar until you have a stiff and glossy meringue.

Gradually mix the icing sugar and almond mixture into the meringue, folding it in with a rubber spatula. Once it has been incorporated, you should have a batter with a slow dropping consistency.

Put the mixture into a piping bag with a 1–1.5cm nozzle and pipe it on to the rounds, trying to keep them as uniform as possible. The easiest way is to hold the nozzle in the centre of the round and stop piping when it reaches the edge of your drawn circle. Leave them to stand for at least 20 minutes to allow a skin to develop – this may take longer.

Before you put the macarons into the oven, drop the tray sharply on to your work surface to help get rid of any air bubbles.

Bake the macarons in the oven for about 12 minutes. They are ready if they peel straight off the parchment when you slide a metal spatula underneath them. Remove them from the oven and transfer them to a rack to cool.

To make the buttercream, beat the butter until fluffy. Add the marmalade, zest and orange blossom water and beat again to mix. Gradually add the icing sugar, continuing to beat until it is all incorporated and the icing is light and creamy. Pipe small amounts of the buttercream on to half of the macarons and sandwich them together with those remaining. Store in an airtight container. To enjoy the macarons at their best, leave them to rest for 24 hours.

PORTUGUESE CUSTARD TARTS

They say that the reason the Portuguese have so many desserts based on egg yolks is because traditionally nuns did all the baking. They used egg whites to starch their wimples, then what did they do with the yolks? They baked these lovely tarts.

MAKES 12

250ml whole milk

1 vanilla pod, split

1 strip of thinly pared orange or lemon peel

35g plain flour

200g caster sugar

3 egg yolks

butter, for greasing

375g pack of ready-rolled puff pastry

First make the custard. Put the milk in a saucepan with the vanilla pod and citrus peel. Heat until the milk is almost at boiling point, then take it off the heat and leave it to cool and infuse.

Put the flour in a bowl and whisk in a third of the milk to make a thin batter. Put the pan with the rest of the milk back over the heat and bring it almost to boiling point again. Pour the milk and flour batter into the heated milk and whisk vigorously for a couple of minutes until it has thickened. Cover with cling film so a skin doesn't form while you make the sugar syrup.

Put the sugar in a small saucepan with 100ml water. Stir over a low heat until the sugar has dissolved, then simmer for a few minutes until the syrup is at the short-thread stage – this means that if you put a few (cooled) drops on your thumb, it will pull to short threads when you touch your index finger to it. Whisk the sugar syrup into the milk mixture.

Put the egg yolks into a bowl and whisk them lightly to break them up. Strain the milk mixture into a jug, then pour it in a steady trickle over the eggs, whisking as you go, until everything is completely combined. Try to make sure the mixture doesn't get too frothy. Cover the custard with cling film again, making sure it is touching the surface, to prevent a skin forming.

Preheat the oven to 250°C/Fan 230°C/Gas 9. Generously butter a 12-hole muffin tray. Take the pastry out of its packet and unroll it. Discard the paper lining, then roll the pastry up again as tightly as you can. Cut the roll into 12 even rounds.

Put a piece of pastry into each of the holes in the muffin tin. Using your fingers, press each one down and out, working it up the sides of the hole. Alternatively, you can simply roll the discs to fit into the holes, but it won't produce quite the same lovely layers of pastry. Pour the cooled custard into the pastry cases, making sure each is filled almost to the top.

Put the tarts in the oven and bake them for 15-20 minutes until the pastry is golden brown, and the top of the custard is slightly scorched. Don't worry if the custard puffs up – it will subside nicely. Allow the tarts to cool before eating them - difficult we know, but they are better cool.

AMERICAN-STYLE PANCAKES *with blueberries*

Pancakes are not just for breakfast and brunch. These are so good you'll want to eat them at any time of day. They make a great pud so go American-style and make a big stack and enjoy them for your tea.

SERVES 4

450g self-raising flour

1 tsp baking powder

½ tsp cinnamon (optional)

pinch of salt

600ml buttermilk

1 tsp vanilla extract, or seeds scraped from 1 vanilla pod

3 eggs, separated

50g butter, melted, plus extra for frying

300g blueberries

MAPLE BUTTER (optional)

150g butter

pinch of salt

pinch of cinnamon

4 tbsp maple syrup

Put the flour, baking powder and cinnamon in a large bowl and add a pinch of salt. Whisk briefly to remove any lumps, then make a well in the centre. Put the buttermilk in a separate bowl and whisk in the vanilla extract or seeds, the egg yolks and the melted butter. Whisk the egg whites until stiff.

Pour the buttermilk mixture into the flour and whisk until well combined. Add a large spoonful of the egg whites and fold them in with a metal spoon, just to loosen the batter a little. Stir in the rest of the egg whites, trying to preserve as much of the air in the whites as possible, to make a fluffy, bubbly batter.

Heat a small frying pan over a medium heat and brush a little butter over the base. Pour about a ladle of batter into the frying pan and it should spread out over the base. Take a large handful of blueberries and sprinkle them over the pancake. The pancake will rise up around the blueberries as it cooks.

When the pancake has browned on the bottom and is firm enough to flip (by this time it will be cooked more than halfway through), turn it over quickly and cook for another minute on the other side. Remove the pancake from the pan and keep it warm while you make the rest.

For the maple butter, put the softened butter in a bowl with a pinch of salt and cinnamon and whisk until white and fluffy. Gradually whisk in the maple syrup until it is all incorporated.

Serve the pancakes with any extra blueberries, spoonfuls of the maple butter and more maple syrup as well if you like.

CHOCOLATE *and* ORANGE SOUFFLÉS
with Grand Marnier sauce

This is a classy number. Dark chocolate and orange are a favourite combo and you could also make these with orange-flavoured choc. You'll need four 150ml ramekins or six smaller ones.

—————————————————— SERVES 4-6 ——————————————————

25g butter, softened, for greasing

1 tbsp caster sugar, for dusting

150ml whole milk

100ml double cream

150g dark chocolate, broken into pieces

grated zest of 1 orange

3 large eggs, separated

75g caster sugar

15g cornflour

15g plain flour

10g cocoa

GRAND MARNIER SAUCE

300ml orange juice

juice of ½ lemon

100g sugar

2 tbsp Grand Marnier

First prepare the ramekins. Rub softened butter over the insides of the ramekins, then use a pastry brush to go over it with upward strokes; this helps the soufflés rise. Dust the insides with the sugar until well coated. Leave the ramekins in the freezer until you need them.

Put the milk in a saucepan and warm it almost to boiling point. Remove the pan from the heat and set it aside. In a separate pan, heat the cream and when it is blood temperature, remove the pan from the heat and add the chocolate. Let the chocolate melt completely, then beat until thick and glossy. Stir in the orange zest and set the mixture aside to cool.

Whisk the yolks with 50g of the sugar until creamy. Sieve the cornflour, plain flour and cocoa into a bowl, then sprinkle this mixture over the egg yolks and sugar and beat until smooth. Pour the milk over the egg and sugar mixture, stirring constantly, then tip it all back into the saucepan. Stir over a low heat until the mixture has thickened to a custard, then remove the pan from the heat and leave to cool, whisking regularly to make sure it doesn't develop a skin. Beat in the chocolate and cream mixture.

Preheat the oven to 190°C/Fan 170°C/Gas 5 and put a baking tray in the oven to heat up.

Whisk the egg whites to the soft peak stage, then start beating in the remaining sugar, a teaspoon at a time, until the mixture is stiff and glossy. Add the egg whites to the chocolate mixture a third at a time, folding it in with a metal spoon as carefully as you can so you don't lose too much volume. Incorporate each spoonful fully before adding the next one.

Divide the mixture between the ramekins, making sure each is filled to the top, then scrape a palette knife over the surface to make it perfectly flat. Run your finger around the rim of each ramekin to create a small groove round the top. This will help the soufflés to rise evenly.

Put the ramekins on the preheated baking tray and bake for 16-18 minutes (depending on the size of your ramekins) until well risen with a slight wobble in the middle. You should get a good rise of at least 3-4cm.

For the sauce, put the orange juice, lemon juice and sugar into a saucepan. Heat gently, stirring constantly until the sugar has dissolved, then turn up the heat a little and simmer for a few minutes until it is syrupy - it will thicken a little more as it cools. Stir in the Grand Marnier, a tablespoon at a time. Serve the soufflés immediately with the sauce on the side to pour into the centre.

CHOCOLATE MOUSSE

This is a hugely popular pud and one of the most often ordered in restaurants. Make your own with really good chocolate and pop them on the table to the delight of young and old.

SERVES 4

125g dark chocolate (at least 70% cocoa solids)

4 eggs, separated

50g icing sugar

25ml rum (optional)

150ml whipping cream

grated chocolate, to garnish

extra cream, to serve (optional)

Break up the chocolate and put it in a heatproof bowl. Set the bowl over a saucepan of barely simmering water, making sure that the bottom of the bowl doesn't touch the water.

When the chocolate has melted, take the pan off the heat and beat in the egg yolks one at a time, then add the icing sugar and the rum, if using. Don't worry if the mixture begins to look grainy when you start adding the egg yolks – it will be smoother by the time you have incorporated the rum and sugar. It will be quite thick at this point.

Whisk the cream until it is full of air but still fairly soft. Fold the cream into the chocolate mixture, until it is completely combined. Whisk the egg whites until they form stiff peaks. Loosen the chocolate mixture with a tablespoon or so of the whites, then fold in the rest, trying to keep as much of the air in them as possible. You should end up with a slightly bubbly but still pourable mixture.

Divide the mixture between 6 ramekins and chill them for several hours until set. They should be firm to touch. Decorate each one with grated chocolate and a little extra cream if you like.

QUEEN OF PUDDINGS

We have fond memories of eating this as children and it's one of the great British puds. In our new version, the custard is thickened with breadcrumbs as usual but it's topped with some gently cooked spiced plums instead of jam. A real aristocrat of a pud.

SERVES 6

CUSTARD

50g butter, plus extra for greasing

400ml whole milk

200ml double cream

1 vanilla pod, split

3 egg yolks

50g caster sugar

100g breadcrumbs

1 tsp lemon zest

PLUM COMPOTE

300g plums, stoned and roughly chopped

zest and juice of ½ orange

pinch of ground ginger

pinch of cinnamon

1 tbsp caster sugar

MERINGUE

3 egg whites

pinch of salt

150g caster sugar

1 tsp cornflour

1 tsp white wine vinegar

Preheat the oven to 150°C/Fan 130°C/Gas 2. Butter a 1-litre ovenproof dish.

Put the butter, milk and cream in a saucepan with the vanilla pod and heat until almost boiling. Remove the pan from the heat, then strain the mixture into a jug.

Whisk the egg yolks in a bowl with the sugar, then pour the milk over them and stir to combine. Add the breadcrumbs and lemon zest, then pour everything into the dish. Bake in the oven for 20-25 minutes until the custard is set; it should still have a wobble in the middle. Allow to cool.

To make the plum compote, put the plums, orange zest and juice, spices and sugar in a saucepan. Heat gently, until the plums soften and start to break down. Strain off most of the excess liquid and leave the plums to cool before spooning them over the cooked custard. Turn the oven up to 180°C/Fan 160°C/Gas 4.

To make the meringue, whisk the egg whites with a pinch of salt until they form soft peaks. Gradually beat in the sugar until the meringues are thick and glossy. Mix the cornflour and vinegar together in a small bowl, then stir this into the meringue.

Spoon or pipe the meringue over the custard and plums, making sure you make plenty of small peaks for some contrast in textures. Put the pud back in the oven for 15-20 minutes until golden brown. Serve hot or cold.

CLAFOUTIS

This is a very traditional French dessert and it's customary to leave the pits in the cherries as they add extra almond flavour. But if you're worried about Auntie Beryl breaking a tooth on one, pit the cherries before adding them.

SERVES 4

500g cherries (pitted or not – up to you)

2 tbsp caster sugar

2 tbsp kirsch or similar cherry liqueur

20g butter, softened, for greasing

1 tbsp ground almonds, for dusting

1 tsp caster sugar

1 tbsp icing sugar, for dusting

BATTER

30g plain flour

30g ground almonds

200ml milk

100ml single cream

25g butter, melted

a few drops of almond extract (optional)

2 eggs

1 tsp lemon zest

Put the cherries in a bowl and sprinkle over the 2 tablespoons of caster sugar and the kirsch. Leave them to macerate for a couple of hours.

Preheat the oven to 180°C/Fan 160°C/Gas 4. Butter a shallow, ovenproof dish. Mix the tablespoon of ground almonds and teaspoon of sugar together, then sprinkle this over the butter. Tap out any excess.

To make the batter, mix the flour and ground almonds in a bowl, making sure there are no lumps. Put the milk, single cream, melted butter and almond extract, if using, in a jug, then whisk to combine.

Make a well in the centre of the flour and almond mixture and break in the eggs. Slowly work the eggs into the dry ingredients until you have a thick paste, then very gradually start adding the milk and cream mixture until you have incorporated it all and have a smooth batter. Stir in the lemon zest.

Arrange the cherries over the base of the dish, along with any juices, then pour over the batter. Bake in the oven for about 30 minutes, by which time the batter should be golden brown and slightly puffed up – it will subside when it cools.

Remove the dish from the oven and allow the clafoutis to cool slightly, before dusting it with icing sugar. Serve hot or cold, with some double cream if you like.

ROSE *and* PISTACHIO ICE CREAM
with gazelle horns

We made this exotic ice cream in a Moroccan hamam in 40-degree heat when we were filming, so it should be a cinch at home. It goes beautifully with the gazelle horn pastries opposite. For the best colour, rub the skins off the pistachios – or buy nibbed pistachios which are already skinned.

SERVES 6

200g pistachios, plus extra for garnish

600ml milk

75g sugar

6 egg yolks

300ml double cream

1–3 tsp rose water

candied rose petals, for garnish

Put the pistachios in a large frying pan and toast them very lightly for a couple of minutes. Leave the pistachios to cool, then grind them as finely as possible in a food processor.

Put the pistachios in a saucepan with the milk and 40g of the sugar and heat until the sugar has dissolved. Allow the milk to come almost to boiling point, then remove the pan from the heat, cover, and leave to infuse. Leave the mixture for at least an hour for a good flavour, or overnight if you can.

Strain the milk and pistachio mixture thoroughly, then reheat, again to just below boiling point. Put the egg yolks in a bowl with the remaining sugar and whisk until the mixture is light and mousse-like. Pour the infused milk over the egg yolks, stirring to combine, then pour everything back into the saucepan. Stir over a very low heat until the mixture is the consistency of a fairly thin custard. If you are worried about the mixture curdling, you can pour the mixture into a bowl and place it over a pan of simmering water, then stir.

Remove the custard from the heat and leave it to cool down. Chill thoroughly, then pour in the double cream. Mix to combine then gradually add the rose water, tasting as you go.

Churn the mixture in an ice cream maker, then put it in the freezer for a couple of hours before serving. If you don't have an ice cream maker, freeze the mixture in a plastic box and whisk at regular intervals to get air into it. Continue until it is too hard to work. Serve garnished with candied rose petals and chopped pistachios.

GAZELLE HORNS

PASTRY

250g plain flour

pinch of salt

1 egg

60g butter, melted

2–3 tsp water or orange blossom water

beaten egg, for sealing

PISTACHIO MARZIPAN FILLING

200g pistachios

75g icing sugar

50g butter, melted and cooled

orange blossom water, to taste

TO FINISH

orange blossom water

icing sugar

The proper name for these Moroccan sweet treats is 'kaab el ghazal'. They're made of a super-delicate pastry, filled with a pistachio paste. Be careful about over filling them as the mixture will expand as it bakes.

First make the pastry. Put the flour in a bowl with the salt and make a well in the centre. Break the egg into the well and start whisking it in with a fork. Gradually add in the melted butter and a little water or orange blossom water – just enough to give you a firm dough. Turn the dough out on to your work surface and knead until smooth – you shouldn't need any flour. If the dough feels dry and is cracking, wet your hands and coat the surface, then continue kneading. When the dough is smooth and elastic, put it in a bowl, cover it with cling film and leave to rest for an hour.

To make the filling, grind the pistachios in a food processor with the sugar until fine, then mix with the butter and a little water or orange blossom water to make a paste. Preheat the oven to 170°C/Fan 150°C/Gas 3½.

Divide the pastry into 4 pieces and roll it out as thinly as you can. You can do this with a pasta roller if you like. Take a piece at a time and cut out 8cm rounds, using the fluted end of a cookie cutter. Place a teaspoon-sized piece of the filling in the centre of each round and fold over into a crescent, sealing the edges with beaten egg. Repeat until you've used all the pastry and filling.

Put the pastries on a baking tray and brush them with egg. You can use a sharp needle to make holes for a design on the top if you like. Bake for 10–15 minutes. The pastry should be cooked through, but just starting to turn a very light brown and still soft to touch – it will firm up when it comes out of the oven. Sprinkle with orange blossom water and dust with icing sugar and serve with the ice cream.

BLACK FOREST PAVLOVA

A Black Forest gâteau is one of those things that just works and so is pavlova. Put these two treats together and you have a taste sensation. Truly lush.

5 large egg whites

250g caster sugar

30g cocoa powder

1 tsp white wine vinegar

50g dark chocolate, grated

CHERRIES

500g cherries, half pitted, half unpitted and with stalks attached

1 tbsp caster sugar

1 tbsp kirsch

50g dark chocolate

TO ASSEMBLE

300ml double cream

1 tbsp icing sugar

25g dark chocolate, shaved or grated (optional)

Preheat the oven to 180°C/Fan 160°C/Gas 4. Line a baking tray with baking parchment and draw a 23cm circle on it. Whisk the egg whites until they reach the soft peak stage. Add the sugar gradually, a tablespoon at a time to start with, then slightly more. Beat in between each addition until the meringue is stiff and glossy. Sieve the cocoa over the top and stir it in until incorporated, then sprinkle over the vinegar and grated chocolate. Stir again so you have a chocolate-flecked meringue.

Use a few tiny blobs of the meringue to secure the parchment to the baking tray, then pile the rest into the marked circle. Make a slight indentation in the middle and allow the meringue to come to peaks around the edges.

Put the meringue in the oven and then turn the temperature down to 150°C/ Fan 130°C/Gas 2. Bake for 1 hour and 15 minutes to 1 hour and 30 minutes. The meringue should be crisp round the edges but with some give in the middle. Turn off the oven and leave the meringue inside to cool completely.

Meanwhile macerate the pitted cherries. Put them in a bowl, then sprinkle over the sugar and kirsch. Turn them over lightly with a spoon, then leave to stand for an hour.

Melt the chocolate. Take the unpitted cherries and make sure they are completely dry. Dip the cherries in the chocolate so they are half covered. Put each cherry on a non-stick surface for the chocolate to harden.

Whisk the cream with the icing sugar to the soft peak stage. Drain the cherries and stir through any of the juices into the cream. Pile the cream over the pavlova, followed by the pitted, macerated cherries. Garnish the pavlova with the chocolate-coated cherries and add a few extra shavings of chocolate on top if you like.

LEMON ICE BOX PIE

This is so much simpler to make than a classic lemon tart and it tastes beyond scrumptious. It's great for a party as you can make it ahead of time and stash it away in the freezer until your guests arrive. Frozen eggstacy!

BASE

200g digestive or gingernut biscuits

50g butter, melted

FILLING

397g can of condensed milk

150ml lemon juice (about 4 lemons)

zest of 2 lemons, plus extra to garnish

5 egg yolks

TOPPING

200ml double cream

1 tbsp icing sugar

Preheat the oven to 170°C/Fan 150°C/Gas 3½. Crush the biscuits to the texture of fine breadcrumbs, then stir in the melted butter. Press the mixture into the base of a round pie dish or a loose-bottomed flan tin - 18cm in diameter is about right.

Pour the condensed milk into a bowl and whisk it with the lemon juice and zest. Beat in the egg yolks, then pour the mixture over the biscuit base.

Bake the tart in the oven for about 20 minutes, until just set. It may still have a wobble in the centre and that's fine.

Leave the pie to cool, then put it in the freezer for several hours. Transfer it from the freezer to the fridge about half an hour before you want to serve it. Whisk the double cream with the icing sugar until thick and billowy. Either pile it on top of the pie or serve it on the side. Decorate the pie with extra lemon zest if you like.

WELSH CAKES *with Welsh whisky*

Welsh cakes are great anyway but when they're made with whisky they go to another level of deliciousness. We baked these in a showground near Aberystwyth and they went down a storm with the locals. Welsh whisky is great but any kind will do.

───────────────── MAKES 20 ─────────────────

100g dried cherries

100ml Welsh whisky
(or any other kind)

250g self-raising flour,
plus extra for dusting

50g caster sugar, plus
extra for coating

pinch of salt

125g butter, chilled and
diced

1 tsp orange zest

1 egg

lard or butter, for
greasing

If your dried cherries are particularly large, cut them up with scissors to the size of currants. Put them in a saucepan and pour in the whisky. Heat until the whisky starts to boil, then remove the pan from the heat and leave the cherries to infuse for an hour.

Put the self-raising flour and caster sugar in a bowl with a pinch of salt. Add the butter and rub it in with your fingers until the mixture resembles fine breadcrumbs. Add the orange zest and the cherries, along with any liquid that they haven't absorbed. Beat the egg and cut it into the mixture with a knife, then as soon as the mixture starts coming together into a dough, work it into a ball with your fingers.

Turn the dough out on to a floured work surface and roll it out to a thickness of ½–1cm. Cut out rounds of 6cm in diameter, then re-roll the leftover dough and repeat. You should get about 20 cakes.

Heat a griddle pan or a heavy frying pan and brush the surface with a little lard or butter. Cook the Welsh cakes in batches over a medium heat, for 2–3 minutes on each side. Make sure the heat isn't too high or the cakes will burn before they are cooked through.

Sprinkle the extra caster sugar on a plate. When the cakes are firm to touch and a deep golden brown, turn them out on to the sugar and flip them over so they are well covered. These are best eaten while hot.

COFFEE *and* WALNUT BUNDT CAKE

A Bundt cake is baked in a Bundt tin and is a mega ring of deliciousness. Coffee and walnut are a perfect flavour partnership and just right with a cup of frothy cappuccino.

450g plain flour

1 tsp baking powder

½ tsp bicarbonate of soda

2 tbsp instant espresso powder

large pinch of salt

225g butter, softened

225 soft light brown sugar

4 eggs

150ml soured cream

1 tsp vanilla extract

100ml strong coffee

100g walnuts, chopped, plus extra to decorate

GLAZE

1 tbsp instant espresso powder

100g icing sugar

Preheat the oven to 170°C/Fan 150°C/Gas 3½. Grease a deep Bundt tin and sprinkle it with flour or use cake release spray if you have some.

Put the flour, baking powder, bicarbonate of soda and espresso powder into a bowl with a large pinch of salt and then whisk to get rid of any lumps. Beat the butter and sugar together in a stand mixer or in a bowl with electric beaters until they have increased in volume and are very soft. Add the eggs, one at a time, following each one with 2 tablespoons of the flour mixture, until they are all incorporated. Fold in the rest of the flour – the mixture will be quite stiff at this stage.

Mix the soured cream, vanilla extract and coffee together, then gradually incorporate this into the batter. Finally, stir in the walnuts.

Pour the batter into the prepared tin and bake for about an hour, checking after 50 minutes. The cake is done when it has shrunk away from the sides, is well risen and a rich brown in colour. Test with a skewer to make sure – it should come out virtually clean.

Leave the cake to cool in the tin for at least half an hour, then turn it out on to a cooling rack.

To make the glaze, dissolve the espresso powder in a tablespoon of just-boiled water, then gradually stir in the icing sugar. Add a few more drops of hot water if necessary, but be sparing as this icing can go from the right consistency to too runny in an instant. You need to be able to spread it, rather than have it run off the cake. When the cake is completely cool, drizzle the icing over it. Decorate with extra walnuts.

BASICS

PERFECT SCRAMBLED EGGS

10g butter

2 eggs

25ml milk, single
cream or crème fraiche
(depending on how
rich you like your eggs)

chopped chives
(optional)

sea salt and freshly
ground black pepper

Melt the butter in a small saucepan or frying pan – non-stick is best as it's much easier to clean. Break the eggs into a bowl, add your choice of milk, cream or crème fraiche and season. Whisk lightly to break up the eggs and combine them with the milk, cream or crème fraiche.

When the butter is foaming but not starting to brown, pour in the eggs. Cook them over a low to medium heat – stirring regularly and leaving them to set for a few seconds in between each stirring – until they are almost cooked to your liking. It's important to remove the pan from the heat just before the eggs get to the stage you want, as they will continue to cook for a few moments. Transfer to a plate immediately and garnish with a few finely chopped chives if you like.

PERFECT FRIED EGG

10g butter

1 egg

Melt the butter in a non-stick frying pan until it is foaming but not brown. Crack the egg into a ramekin, then pour it into the butter, trying to make sure the white doesn't spread out too much. Cook the egg gently over a low heat until it's done to your liking.

If you want a very runny yolk and the white around it isn't quite setting, you can help it along by either putting a lid on the pan, or by spooning some of the hot butter over the egg.

For an over-easy egg, as soon as the underside of the white is cooked, flip the whole thing over, trying very hard not to break the yolk. Leave it for another 10 seconds or so for the whites to set around the yolk. Serve immediately while piping hot.

PERFECT POACHED EGG

1 tsp white wine
vinegar

1 egg

Half fill a saucepan with water, and add the vinegar. Bring the water to the boil, then carefully lower the egg (still in its shell) into the water and leave it for 20 seconds exactly. Remove the egg from the water.

Turn the heat down so the water is barely simmering. Carefully crack the egg into the water and cook it for 3 minutes. Once the egg is cooked it will rise to the surface. Remove the egg from the pan and put it on some kitchen paper to drain before serving.

PERFECT BOILED EGG

SERVES 1

1 egg (at room
temperature)

Bring a saucepan of water to the boil. When it's bubbling furiously, put the egg on a spoon and lower it gently into the water. Have a timer ready as well as a bowl of cold water so you can stop the eggs cooking immediately you remove them from the pan.

For a just-set white and runny yolk, cook the egg for $4\frac{1}{2}$ minutes. For a completely set white with a runny yolk, cook for 5 minutes. For a set white and a partially set yolk (an oeuf mollet) cook for 6 minutes – 7 minutes will make the yolk very slightly fudgier. For a just hard-boiled egg with a deep yellow yolk and no hint of greyness around its rim, cook for 8 minutes. When your egg is done to your liking, plunge it into cold water to stop it cooking, then eat at once.

MAYONNAISE

2 egg yolks

1 tsp mustard

250ml sunflower or groundnut oil

squeeze of lemon juice or a few drops of vinegar

sea salt and freshly ground black pepper

Put the egg yolks in a bowl with the mustard and a little salt. Mix them together until well combined.

Start drizzling in the oil, a few drops at a time, whisking constantly, until the mixture has thickened. Keep adding the oil, very gradually, until you have incorporated it all. If the mayonnaise seems to be becoming greasy or too thick to work with, add a few drops of warm water and whisk thoroughly before adding any more oil.

Taste the mayonnaise, then add more seasoning and a squeeze of lemon or a few drops of vinegar if you think it needs some acidity.

GARLIC MAYONNAISE

To make garlic mayonnaise, finely chop 2 garlic cloves and mash them to a paste with a little salt. Put this in a bowl with the egg yolks and mustard, mix well until combined and proceed as above.

PANCAKE BATTER

125g plain flour
pinch of salt
1 egg
300ml milk
25g butter

Put the flour in a bowl with a pinch of salt. Whisk it lightly to get rid of any lumps, then make a well in the centre. Break the egg into a ramekin and pour it into the well. Using a small whisk, gradually start combining the egg with the flour, working in from the sides until you have a very thick paste. Trickle in the milk a little at a time, whisking constantly until the batter is lump free, then add the rest of the milk. Set the batter aside to rest for about an hour.

When you're ready to use the batter, melt the butter in a frying pan and pour most of it into the batter. Give it a quick whisk and use as required.

PROPER CUSTARD

250ml whole milk
250ml double cream
1 vanilla pod, split or 1 tsp vanilla extract
1 coffee bean (optional)
6 egg yolks
50g caster sugar

Put the milk and the cream in a saucepan with the vanilla pod or extract and the coffee bean, if using (it adds depth of flavour but doesn't make the custard taste of coffee). Bring the milk and cream almost to the boil, then remove the pan from the heat and set it aside for the flavours to infuse while the mixture cools.

Whisk the egg yolks and sugar together in a bowl until pale and foamy. Reheat the milk and cream, again to just below boiling point. Strain the milk mixture through a sieve into a jug and rinse out the saucepan. Slowly pour the milk mixture over the eggs, whisking constantly as you do so, then pour it all back into the saucepan. Set the pan over a very low heat and stir constantly until the custard has thickened slightly and you can draw a line through it when it coats the back of a spoon.

Strain the custard again and if you aren't using it immediately, put the vanilla pod back into it. Cover the custard with cling film, making sure the cling film comes into contact with the surface to prevent a skin forming, and leave it to cool.

BASIC VANILLA ICE CREAM

300ml whole milk

300ml double cream

2 vanilla pods, split,
or 2 tsp vanilla extract

4 egg yolks

100g caster sugar

Put the milk and the cream in a saucepan with the vanilla pods or extract. Bring it almost to the boil, then remove the pan from the heat and set it aside for the flavours to infuse while the mixture cools.

Have a bowl of ice-cold water ready to chill the custard down once you are happy with the thickness. Whisk the egg yolks and sugar together in a bowl until pale and foamy. Reheat the milk and cream, again until just below boiling point. Strain the milk mixture through a sieve into a jug and rinse out the saucepan. Slowly pour the milk mixture over the eggs, whisking constantly as you do so, then pour it all back into the saucepan. Set the pan over a very low heat and stir constantly until the custard has thickened slightly and you can draw a line through it when it coats the back of a spoon.

Plunge the pan into the bowl of iced water to stop the custard cooking. Cover the custard with cling film to stop a skin forming, then chill. Stir in the double cream.

If you have an ice cream maker, churn your ice cream, then transfer it to a container and store it in the fridge. If you don't have a machine, pile the mixture into a plastic container and freeze it immediately. Remove and whisk it vigorously every half hour until it has completely set. Fifteen minutes before you want to serve the ice cream, take it out of the freezer and transfer it to the fridge.

LEFTOVER CHICKEN STOCK

MAKES 750ml–1 LITRE

2 onions, unpeeled and quartered

2 carrots, roughly chopped

1 tbsp olive oil

1–3 chicken carcasses, including any skin

1 sprig of thyme

2 celery sticks, roughly chopped

a few peppercorns

1 bay leaf

parsley stems

This is a great stock to make with your roast chicken carcass. You can save a few carcasses up in the freezer to make a large quantity of stock. Preheat the oven to its highest temperature. Put the onion and carrot in a roasting tin and drizzle them with oil, then roast them until they are starting to char. Alternatively, you can do this in a pan on the hob. The idea is to caramelise the vegetables to enrich the stock.

Break the chicken carcasses up a little, then put them in a saucepan with the remaining ingredients and cover with water. Use up to a litre for 1 carcass and up to 1.5 litres for 2 or 3, but don't add so much water that the chicken is floating around. It needs to be quite a snug fit. Bring the water to the boil and skim off any mushroom-coloured foam that collects on top. Keep skimming until the foam turns white, then turn down the heat and cover the pan. Simmer the stock very gently for $1\frac{1}{2}$–2 hours.

Strain the stock through a sieve lined with kitchen paper or muslin, but don't push the bits through if you want a clear stock. Discard all the solids. Leave the stock to cool to room temperature, then chill it in the fridge. When it is cold, you can remove any fat that's sitting on top.

You can store the stock in the fridge for up to 4 days, or freeze it. You can also reduce it down further to get a more concentrated flavour and freeze it in ice cube trays. Once frozen, turn the cubes out into a large bag or plastic container.

STOCK *from* SCRATCH

several raw chicken
backs or carcasses and
4 wings

or 1kg chicken wings

1 large onion, unpeeled
and quartered

1 large carrot, roughly
chopped

2 celery sticks

2 bay leaves

a few black peppercorns

a sprig of thyme

a sprig of parsley

a few garlic cloves

This stock is made from raw chicken, rather than cooked, and has extra
depth of flavour and a lovely texture.

Put the chicken into a large saucepan or stockpot. Cover it with plenty of
cold water –the water should come to about 3cm above the chicken. Bring
the water to the boil, then keep skimming off the mushroom-coloured foam
that appears until it turns white. Add all the remaining ingredients, partially
cover the pan and simmer the stock gently for about 3 hours until it is a
rich golden brown.

Strain the stock through a sieve lined with kitchen paper or muslin, but
don't push the bits through if you want a clear stock. Discard all the solids.
Leave the stock to cool to room temperature, then chill it in the fridge.
When it is cold, you can remove any fat that's sitting on top.

You can store the stock in the fridge for up to 4 days, or freeze it. You
can also reduce it down further to get a more concentrated flavour and
freeze it in ice cube trays. Once frozen, turn the cubes out into a large
bag or plastic container.

SHORTCRUST PASTRY

350g plain flour

200g cold butter,
cut into small cubes

1 egg, beaten with
1 tbsp cold water

To make the pastry, put the flour and butter in a food processor and blend on the pulse setting until the mixture resembles coarse breadcrumbs. Be careful not to over-process or the mixture will start to come together before you add the egg mixture.

With the motor running, add the egg mixture in a slow stream. Stop processing as soon as the mixture starts to come together and is beginning to form a ball – you may not need all the egg and water. Don't process for so long that the mixture forms a firm ball that whizzes round the bowl – this will stretch the pastry too much.

Remove the dough from the processor, gathering it together with your fingertips. Shape it into a flattened ball or square, bearing in mind the shape you're going to be rolling.

If you prefer to make your pastry by hand, put the flour in a bowl, add the cubes of butter and rub them into the flour with your fingertips until the mixture resembles coarse breadcrumbs. Keep lifting the mixture out of the bowl as you rub in the fat to get as much air into the pastry as possible. Add the egg and water and stir it in with a round-bladed knife until the dough comes together. Shape the dough into a ball as before. This makes enough pastry for a double-crust pie.

CHICKEN WRAP *with* GUACAMOLE

1 tsp olive oil

1 tsp chipotle paste

50g cooked chicken, shredded or sliced

pinch of cumin

juice of ½ lime

2 tbsp guacamole

1 large lettuce leaf, shredded

1 slice red onion, finely chopped

1 wrap

a few coriander leaves

sea salt and freshly ground black pepper

GUACAMOLE

juice of 1 lime

2 ripe avocados, diced

1 small red onion, finely chopped

2 medium tomatoes, finely diced

a few sprigs of coriander, finely chopped

1 small red chilli, finely chopped

pinch of cumin

To make the guacamole, put the lime juice in a bowl. Add the avocado and turn it in the lime juice immediately. Season with salt and pepper, then mash very briefly so just a few chunks of avocado are broken up. Add the remaining ingredients and stir. This makes more than you need for one sandwich but it will keep in the fridge for a couple of days.

Heat the olive oil in a small frying pan. Add the chipotle paste with a tablespoon of water, then stir to combine. Add the chicken and cumin, then fry for a couple of minutes over a high heat until the chicken is well coated with the paste and is starting to turn brown in places. Remove the pan from the heat, tip the chicken mixture into a bowl and set it aside to cool. Squeeze over the lime juice and season with salt and pepper.

Arrange the guacamole, chicken, lettuce and onion down the centre of the wrap and garnish with coriander leaves. Fold the 2 ends of the wrap over the filling, then roll it up. Cut it in half and serve or wrap tightly in foil if you're going to eat it later.

CLASSIC CHICKEN *and* BACON SANDWICH

2 thick slices of bread

butter

1 tbsp mayonnaise

½ tsp wholegrain mustard

2 cornichons, finely chopped

4 slices of chicken

2 slices of bacon, grilled

1 tomato, sliced

1 large lettuce leaf, shredded

You need good-quality, fairly soft bread for this. Granary works well but sourdough is not suitable. Butter the bread.

Mix the mayonnaise with the mustard and cornichons and spread the mixture over one slice of bread. Lay the chicken on top, then follow with the bacon, tomato and lettuce. Top with the remaining slice of bread and gently press it all down. Cut the sandwich in half and serve.

CHOPPED CHICKEN SANDWICH

50g chicken, chopped

½ celery stick, finely diced

1 spring onion, finely chopped

1 tbsp mayonnaise

a few tarragon leaves, finely chopped

squeeze of lemon juice

butter

2 thick slices of bread

handful of watercress leaves

sea salt and freshly ground pepper

Breast is best for this sandwich. Put the chicken in a bowl with the celery and spring onion, then season with salt and pepper. Mix the mayonnaise with the tarragon leaves and lemon juice, then add this to the bowl with the chicken and stir to combine thoroughly.

Butter the bread and pile the chicken on one piece. Top with lots of peppery watercress and the other slice of bread. Cut in half and serve.

CURRIED CHICKEN BAGUETTE

2 tsp oil

100g leftover chicken curry

OR 100g leftover chicken, shredded and 1 tsp medium curry powder

2 tbsp yoghurt

1 tbsp mango chutney

handful of coriander, finely chopped

a few slices of red onion

1 tbsp lemon juice

hunk of baguette or a crusty roll

a few lettuce leaves (iceberg is probably best), shredded

sea salt and freshly ground black pepper

This works well with any leftover chicken curry, especially the drier sort. Heat the oil in a frying pan and add the chicken curry or the shredded chicken and the curry powder. Fry the chicken until heated through and crisp. Put the yoghurt in a bowl and season it with salt and pepper, then stir in the mango chutney and coriander. Allow the chicken to cool a little, then add it to the yoghurt.

Put the slices of red onion in a bowl and toss them with the lemon juice and a good pinch of salt. Tear open the baguette or roll and add plenty of lettuce. Pile the chicken mixture on top of the lettuce then top with red onion. Yum!

TECHNIQUES

Here are a few little tips you might find helpful when cooking with eggs and chicken.

SEPARATING EGGS

For quite a few of the recipes in this book you need to separate eggs and use only the yolks or whites so it's good to hone your technique. It's particularly important to get the whites clear, as even a little bit of yolk creeping in makes them hard to whisk successfully. Some white in with the yolks isn't so much of a problem.

You need 2 nice clean bowls. Crack the egg, holding it over a bowl, and let the white dribble into the bowl, while holding the yolk in one half of the shell. Carefully tip the egg from one half shell to the other so the rest of the white drips into the bowl, then drop the yolk into the second bowl.

BRINING

Some people swear by brining to keep chicken lovely and moist and tender; others think it makes no difference. We sometimes like to brine our chicken and this is what we do.

2 chicken breasts or 4 thighs

50g sea salt

100g caster sugar

Dissolve the sugar and salt in 6 cups of lukewarm water in a large bowl, then add the chicken. Cover the bowl with cling film and put it in the fridge for at least 2 hours.

If you want a brine a whole chicken, use 50 grams of salt per litre of water if brining overnight. If brining for less than 4 hours, use 100 grams of salt per litre of water.

VELVETING

This is a popular trick in Chinese cooking and helps to prevent chicken from becoming dry and overcooked when stir-fried. It also gives it an authentic Chinese texture.

4 chicken breasts, sliced into strips

1 egg white

2 tsp cornflour

Put the chicken strips in a bowl. Whisk together the egg white and cornflour, making as smooth a paste as you can. Pour this mixture over the chicken and stir thoroughly so the chicken is completely coated. Chill for 20 minutes in the fridge.

JOINTING A CHICKEN

Buying a whole chicken and cutting it into breasts, thighs and drumsticks can be far cheaper than buying chicken pieces – and you have the carcass and trimmings to use for delicious home-made stock. You can ask your butcher to joint your chicken for you. but it is useful to know how to do it yourself. Use a good sharp knife, take things slowly and gently and be careful.

1. Place the chicken breast-side up on your work surface. Take off any trussing string. To remove the leg, first slice into the skin where the thigh joins the body.

2. Now pull the leg out away from the body and you will see the bone. Ease it away from its socket, then slice around it to remove the leg from the carcass.

3. Repeat to remove the other leg, again pulling it away from the body to expose the bone and slicing through to release it.

4. To remove the breast fillets, first feel along the breast bone with your fingers. Using a sharp knife, cut down along the side of the breastbone, staying as close to the bone as you can so you don't lose any meat.

1   2   3   4

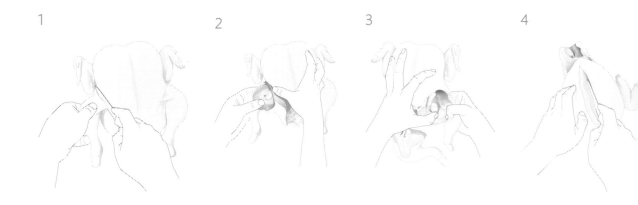

5. Using sweeping motions with your knife, continue cutting the breast away to release it from the bone. Repeat with the other breast

6. Cut off the little wing bone from each breast where the wing joint meets the breast.

7. Slice the breast fillets in half if you like.

8. To separate the thigh and drumstick, place the leg skin-side down, find where the bone meets the socket, then cut through between the joint. Repeat with the other leg.

5   6

7   8

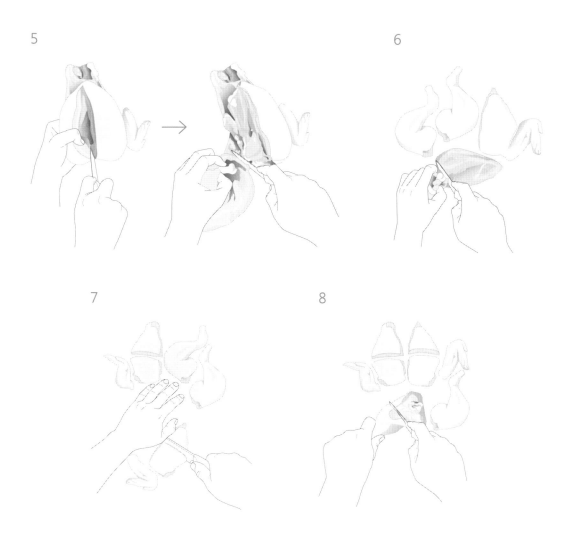

BUTTERFLYING A CHICKEN BREAST

Chicken breasts can be quite chunky in places and butterflying - slicing them in half - makes them an even thickness so they cook more evenly all over. This only takes a few moments and is very easy to do.

1. Place the chicken breast on your work surface. Take a sharp knife and insert it along the long side of the breast.

2. Slice into the breast, but stop just short of the other side.

3. Open out the breast like a book.

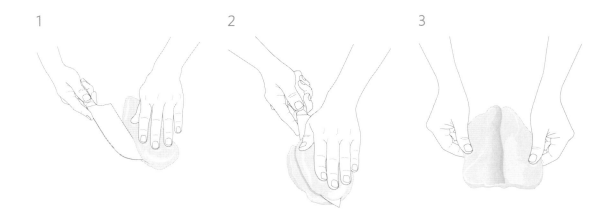

BONING A CHICKEN THIGH

Chicken thighs have good tasty, juicy meat. They can stand long cooking or can also be quickly grilled or pan-fried. For some dishes, thighs need to be boneless and it is easy to remove the bones yourself.

1. Place the thigh skin-side down and find the bone with your fingers.

2. Take a sharp knife and cut along one side of the bone, leaving as little meat on the bone as possible.

3. Cut down the other side of the bone, again keeping as close to the bone as you can and gently releasing the meat.

4. Get the knife underneath the bone and gently work it along, scraping it away from the meat.

5. Carefully cut the bone away at the end.

6. Now you have your boned thigh. The bone can be saved for stock.

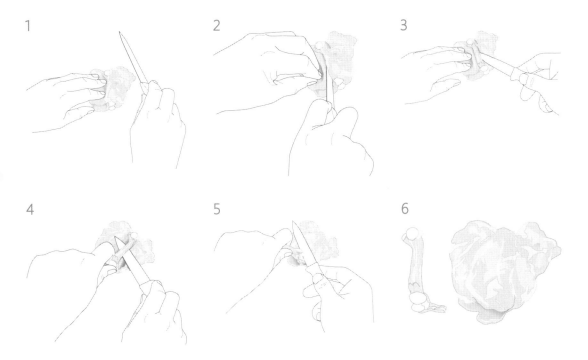

SPATCHCOCKING A CHICKEN

Spatchcocking a chicken means flattening it so that it cooks more quickly on a barbecue or in the oven and you get lots of lovely crispy skin. Great way of having a Sunday roast midweek – see our recipe on page 114.

1. Put the chicken breast-side down on your work surface with the parson's nose facing you. You'll need some poultry shears or sturdy kitchen scissors.

2. With the scissors, cut right along one side of the backbone.

3. Turn the chicken around and cut back down the other side of the backbone.

4. Remove the backbone and set it aside. You can use it for stock.

5. Turn the chicken breast-side up. Put one hand over the breast and press down firmly with your other hand to flatten the chicken as much as you can.

6. Your chicken is spatchcocked and ready to cook.

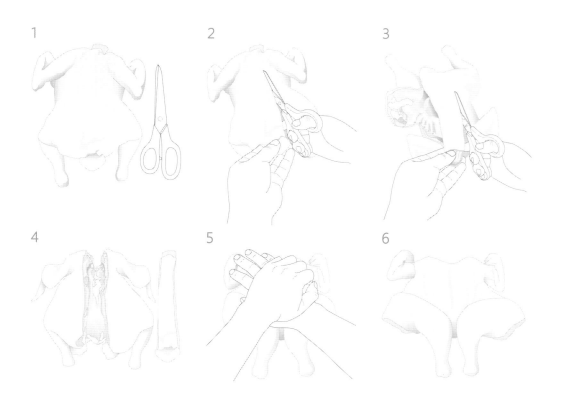

INDEX

What do you get when you cross
a chicken with a guitar?

A chicken that makes music
when you pluck it.

CHEERS GANG

We've had such a great time making this book and there are loads of people we'd like to thank. First off, the talented Catherine Phipps who has inspired us and helped us put together such an amazing selection of recipes. Then there's our mate Andrew Hayes-Watkins who takes photographs to make our mouths water – and he eats all the food and never puts on a gram of weight! Huge thanks to Anna Burgess-Lumden, Lisa Harrison and their assistant Lou Kenney for their tireless efforts in cooking all the food so beautifully for the pictures.

Massive hugs to the wonderful Abi Hartshorne for a super-cool design, to Lucie Stericker for her creative input, and to our faithful editor Jinny Johnson for translating our wildest ramblings. Amanda Harris, our publisher, never fails to support and encourage us – thank you Amanda, we love you.

To Natalie Zietcer, Holly Pye, Sarah Hart, Rowan Lawton, Eugenie Furniss and all at James Grant and Furniss Lawton - you are all totally amazing. Thanks so much for everything you do.

We'd also like to thank all the great people involved in making our television series CHICKEN AND EGG: our executive producer Pete Lawrence, series producer Hannah Corneck and home ec Rob Allison; directors Abdullai Adejumo, Fergus Colville, Becky Pratt and Dick Sharman; assistant producers and researchers Katie Brimblecombe, Rosa Brough, Sophie Burton, Chloé Juyon, Sophie Wogden and Sophia Wollschlanger; production management Amanda Brown, Vicky Knight, Miranda Pincott and Lucy Smith; and crew Jon Boast, Tim Pitot, Richard Hill, Robbie Johnson and Jack Coathupe. It's been a blast.

We would also like to thank our Commissioner, Elliot Reed. And last but not least, on our travels we've met lots of amazing people who've cooked with us, eaten with us and shared their recipes - big thanks to you all.

Lots of love!